EFFECTIVE LEARNING AND T
SCOTTISH SECONDARY SCHO

GUIDANCE

Member of
Plain English Campaign
committed to
clearer communication

27

PEC

A report by HM Inspectors of Schools
The Scottish Office Education and Industry Department

Further Enquiries about this report should be addressed to:

The Scottish Office Education and Industry Department
3-B 06
Victoria Quay
Leith
Edinburgh EH 6 6QQ

Tel 0131 - 244 0652

ISBN 0 7480 3091 3

CONTENTS

FOREWORD

In 1988, HM Inspectors of Schools published the report *Management of Educational Resources: Effective Secondary Schools*. It identified some of the features common to many of the schools which, through inspections over the period 1984 to 1988, were judged to be effective. The report stated that "The quality of guidance provision influences the tone of the whole school. It is of crucial importance in establishing and maintaining an atmosphere in which young people know they are valued as individuals and feel encouraged to learn".

HM Inspectors of Schools have already published a series of eleven reports that aim to identify the features which contribute to effective learning and teaching in specific subjects. This report, the twelfth, falls within that series, but the focus is on effective guidance in a whole-school context rather than on learning and teaching in particular subject departments. It derives from the inspection of guidance in more than 250 schools, and from the monitoring and evaluation of various developments in guidance over the last 10 years.

D A OSLER
HM Senior Chief Inspector of Schools

SUMMARY

1. Introduction

This report presents HM Inspectors' considered views on appropriate aims and effective provision of guidance in secondary schools. It describes and exemplifies approaches which successfully address the needs of pupils in curricular, careers and personal guidance. It reviews the various organisational structures for guidance, the quality of education for personal and social development, and links with parents and the wider community. Important issues relating to the management of guidance are also considered. The report is based on over 250 inspections of guidance in secondary schools and draws on a range of other published reports on various aspects of provision for guidance, including careers education.

2. Historical development, aims and the guidance process

Teachers in Scotland have always recognised that schools have a responsibility for the welfare and well-being of young people as well as for their formal academic education. There has always been help and support available for pupils when educational decisions require to be taken, when a crisis situation arises at school or in the home, and when important decisions have to be taken about obtaining employment or entering further or higher education. Over the last 20 years the notion of the school as a caring community has evolved to include the planned provision of curricular, careers and personal guidance.

In 1986 in *More Than Feelings Of Concern*, the Scottish Central Committee on Guidance identified eight objectives for schools to consider. The first of these aims, "to ensure that each pupil knows and is known personally and in some depth by at least one member of staff", continues to provide the basis for all effective guidance. Building on that essential pre-requisite, the other aims identify specific areas for schools to consider. These include: the provision for aspects of pupils' personal and social development; the response to specific individuals' needs; the development of good links with the home and support agencies; and the effective communication of information relevant to the welfare of individual pupils. These aims of guidance remain as relevant today as they were 10 years ago.

Over the last 10 years, the term 'counselling' has been used in connection with the process of guidance. 'Counselling', as it applies in schools, should not be confused with therapeutic counselling which is properly the preserve of, for example, psychologists, psychotherapists and psychiatrists. However, when individual guidance is at its most effective, it is similar in many respects to the counselling process. It is concerned with good inter-personal relationships which are based on showing respect, listening, empathising and reflecting. The development of counselling skills has become an integral part of all guidance staff training. Most guidance staff build and sustain very good relationships with individual pupils. Many would benefit from some further training in counselling skills, not to establish themselves as counsellors, but to assist them to develop further some of the skills which are particularly helpful in their interaction with pupils and parents.

3. Guidance arrangements in the school context

Because of the wide national range in the nature and size of schools, it is not possible to lay down a uniform pattern of promoted posts in guidance or to assign specific responsibilities to these posts. The total number of guidance posts in schools can vary, not only in relation to the total roll, but also in the way in which senior management choose to deploy staff. Education authorities and headteachers need to consider carefully the rationale behind the deployment of promoted guidance posts.

Education authorities vary in their expectations concerning qualifications and training for guidance. Preliminary training for new appointees to guidance should be a basic requirement, followed by later opportunities for more extensive staff development.

The allocation of time for guidance duties varies significantly between, and sometimes within, schools. Education authorities vary in the extent to which they advise schools about time allocations to guidance, and few authorities monitor closely the arrangements made by schools. The great majority of guidance staff willingly tackle a wide range of duties. In many cases they find it very difficult to undertake these duties within the time allocated. It is, therefore, important that guidance tasks are prioritised within a coherent attempt to manage time effectively.

The quality of accommodation allocated for guidance varies greatly between schools. Much depends on the overall range of accommodation available to each school, but another important factor is the extent to which the school chooses to give some priority to guidance in allocating space. Overall, the majority of schools have a satisfactory range of resources to support most guidance activities.

In their operational structures for guidance, nearly all schools adopt 'horizontal' or 'vertical' structures, or a blend of these two basic organis-ational patterns. Arguments for and against 'horizontal' and 'vertical' systems are identified in the full report. It is the responsibility of individual schools to review their own circumstances and resources with a view to choosing the structure which best meets the needs of its pupils. However, in the light of recent and future developments in Scottish education, the advantages of a vertical structure have become more compelling.

Most schools recognise that to some extent all members of staff are guidance teachers. In addition to the professional expectation that all teachers have a responsibility for addressing their pupils' educational needs, many schools explicitly state that all staff should show concern for the personal and social needs of their pupils. Within a whole school approach to guidance, some schools make specific arrangements for 'first level' guidance. Whether or not schools explicitly refer to 'first level' or whole-school approaches, the guidance team should have a central role with clear lines of communication between guidance teachers and all other staff.

In particular, close links with learning support staff are an essential feature in addressing pupils' needs appropriately and consistently across the curriculum. Regular communication between the guidance team and learning support staff is necessary: to review the learning needs of pupils; to address pupils' social and academic concerns; and to discuss referrals or potential referrals to caring agencies. Within the arrangements for transfer of pupils from primary to secondary education, and in relation to provision for pupils with special educational needs, guidance and learning staff have an important joint role.

4. Personal guidance: pastoral care

A major objective for guidance staff is to ensure that they know each pupil in their case-load as well as possible. A common aim in the job specification of guidance teachers is "to meet each pupil in their case-load at least once per year on a one-to-one basis". This is seen as fundamental in attempting not only to meet the general needs of all pupils but also to identify and address needs which are specific to a particular pupil and which may be of a personal or confidential nature.

The extent to which guidance staff achieve the aim of one-to-one interviews for all pupils each session has often been disappointing. Many schools recognise the value of guidance teachers meeting small groups of three or four pupils to discuss, for example settling into S1 or how the early part of S3 is proceeding. Such arrangements enable guidance staff to prioritise contacts with pupils who appear to require more in-depth individual support.

The links between primary and secondary schools and the smooth transfer from one sector to the other are essential elements in the educational process for all pupils. While primary and secondary schools have long recognised the value of maintaining close links, the introduction of the National Guidelines 5-14 has further emphasised the importance of continuity in pupils' experience as they move from primary to secondary education. Guidance staff are usually closely involved in the process.

Nearly all schools recognise that an essential part of helping pupils to adjust to new surroundings lies in monitoring aspects of attendance, taking appropriate action over absenteeism, and explaining expectations about behaviour. In recent years, guidance staff in most schools have developed more appropriate roles in relation to their involvement in matters of discipline. Their role in disciplinary procedures is more typically that of counselling and support to complement the application of sanctions.

For many years guidance staff have maintained a profile of information designed to assist in the development of a rounded picture of each pupil's academic progress and attainment, social competence, vocational inclinations and interests. Such profile records are invaluable to staff when completing references, assisting pupils with their applications for jobs or for entry to courses at college or university, briefing careers officers or other support agency personnel, or reporting back to parents. In recent sessions, guidance staff in many schools have become involved in various aspects of producing a National Record of Achievement.

5. Curricular guidance

Guidance has a central role in ensuring that all young people achieve their academic potential during secondary education. Effective monitoring of pupils' progress is a basic pre-requisite in creating a situation where guidance staff can assist pupils and their parents at, for example, important transition stages when choice of subjects or courses of study have to be made. Inspection evidence has shown that schools are not consistently effective in monitoring progress; a significant number of schools require to give more attention to this important aspect of guidance, particularly beyond S2.

In most schools there are satisfactory arrangements for liaison between guidance and subject staff in reviewing pupils' progress in S1 and S2. Pupils' expected and actual progress are usually reviewed appropriately throughout S1 and S2. Some schools, however, require to give more attention to monitoring the progress of all pupils at all stages.

In nearly all schools, guidance staff are at the centre of the process through which S2 pupils choose their future subjects. Effective provision for the transition from S2 to S3 includes: a carefully planned series of events, interviews and meetings with parents; a structured teaching programme to assist pupils prepare for option choice; and familiarisation with the careers library. Specific responsibility for this provision should be invested in a member of the guidance or senior management team.

The transition to the upper school, particularly the move from S4 into S5, has assumed greater importance as a period requiring a special guidance focus. Inspection evidence shows that the preparation for option choice in S4/S5 frequently fails to match the quality of provision in S2. There are often only limited opportunities for pupils to discuss their options with their guidance teacher and, in a significant number of schools, the contribution of guidance staff to S4/S5 option choice procedures is minimal.

Increasingly, guidance staff are involved in monitoring the progress and attainment of pupils in the upper school years as they approach national examinations. At this stage, effective guidance continues to be founded on systematic liaison with subject teachers to ensure that pupils' expected and actual progress are compared at regular intervals. While pupils at all stages and their parents should be encouraged to contact guidance staff to discuss any matters of concern, it is particularly important that at the upper stages early action is taken to help with any difficulties.

The successful implementation of the Higher Still development programme will require high quality guidance support for all students. Support currently provided by schools will, in future, need to be adjusted to meet the needs of students following Higher Still programmes.

6. Careers guidance

Careers education is an essential part of guidance provision. Schools have different patterns of providing careers-related activities. The most successful approaches to careers education are found in schools where responsibility for delivering and monitoring the quality of provision is clearly identified; and where senior management and guidance staff co-operate closely to ensure that the various elements of careers education are effectively co-ordinated.

At S1, some schools have established the beginnings of a personal profile which contains early thoughts about future employment linked to self-assessment, awareness of interests, and identification of personal strengths and weaknesses. In S2, virtually all schools provide identifiable elements of careers education and guidance in the processes leading up to curriculum choice for S3 and S4.

In S3 and S4, progressively more attention is given to broadening the pupils' awareness of the range of opportunities open to them in higher education, further education, training and employment. Many schools introduce a computerised interest inventory as part of their provision in S3. Most need to take more account of the fact that effective use of such computer programs requires sufficient time to examine and analyse the reasons for the various suggestions in individual print-outs. Most schools make appropriate arrangements for pupils in S4 and beyond to participate in work experience, attend careers conventions and open days, and to hear speakers on various aspects of industry, commerce, and the professions.

The contribution of careers officers is a significant feature of the careers guidance process. It is important that guidance staff provide appropriate briefing information for careers officers prior to their interviews with pupils in S4 and beyond. In some cases guidance teachers need to be more meticulous in addressing this requirement; and some should be better informed of the various opportunities that are open to school leavers.

At S5 and S6, the range of careers-related activities normally entails further use of computerised and printed careers information packages, opportunities to attend careers conventions, college and university open days and to hear speakers on various aspects of the world of work. In many schools, careers education is enhanced by a useful range of schools-industry liaison activities.

A well-resourced, regularly up-dated and easily accessible careers library is essential. In many schools, responsibility rests with the school librarian whose presence generally ensures that careers resources are used to good effect. A member of the guidance team should liaise regularly with the librarian and the careers officer. Good practice in some schools involves senior pupils in assisting with routine maintenance and daily oversight of the careers information resources.

7. Personal guidance: individual support and counselling

Guidance staff require to deal with personal 'crisis' points which sometimes occur with little warning, as well as with those which arise within the normal pattern of school life. The length of time over which a pupil requires specific support and counselling can be relatively short or encompass the whole of secondary education.

All schools claim that a high priority for guidance staff is the identification of particular needs of individual pupils. This is one of the key objectives of guidance programmes relating to transition points such as P7/S1 and subject/course choice. Individual needs are identified in various other ways, for example through monitoring academic progress, attendance and discipline referrals, or in the preparation of reports to parents. Important information is brought to the attention of guidance staff by parents and outside agency personnel.

The extent to which pupils take the initiative in seeking the help of guidance teachers is an important indicator of the effectiveness of guidance provision in a school and of the confidence which pupils have in their guidance teachers. Some schools have successfully encouraged self-referral.

Recent evidence indicates an increase in the extent and quality of co-operation between guidance staff and teachers involved in the provision of learning and behaviour support (including that for pupils with special educational needs, whether recorded or not). Discussions with learning and behaviour support staff frequently address the very specific pastoral and social needs of pupils whose learning difficulties are very considerable and who, until fairly recently, would have been unlikely to have been in mainstream education. Individual support on all aspects of curricular and careers guidance is a major dimension of guidance provision during secondary education. The range of need can be extensive.

During S1 and S2, an important aspect of individual support relates to the choice of subjects to study during S3 and S4. Beyond S1 and S2, guidance staff are often involved in responding to complex demands associated with curricular and vocational issues. Inspections have indicated that the extent of this aspect of guidance work with individual pupils is increasing as more pupils, representing an ever-widening range of ability, opt to stay on at the S5 and S6 stages.

Individual support and counselling on careers matters increases steadily as pupils progress through secondary education, reaching a peak as final decisions and plans are made about the post-school phase of life. Most schools appropriately support individual pupils over applications for jobs, in the provision of references, in preparation for specific interviews relating to employment or to post-school education, and over entry procedures for colleges and universities.

8. Education for personal and social development

In recent years, national debate on key aspects of the education of young people has emphasised the importance of the 'core skills' of communication, numeracy, personal and interpersonal skills, problem solving and information technology. Drawing on the increased recognition of these important skills and abilities, recent documentation within the Higher Still Development Programme indicates that the development of core skills is a priority. Education for personal and social development must therefore include core skills. Specific programmes in personal and social education (PSE) should have important contributions to make, particularly in the aspects of communication, problem solving and personal and interpersonal skills.

The rationale for the *National Guidelines for Personal and Social Development 5-14* commences with the clear and unequivocal statement that "Personal and social development is a fundamental aspect of the education of the whole child". In education for personal and social development, pupils are encouraged to increase their knowledge and understanding about themselves, others, their immediate environment and the world in which they live.

Clearly, responsibility for implementing these aims cannot, and should not, reside entirely with guidance staff. In planning effective education for personal and social development, schools must consider the implications of the whole school, cross-curricular and special focus approaches advocated in the National Guidelines 5-14.

The potential importance of PSE programmes is not reflected in a consistent quality of provision in schools. Overall, standards are very variable. Provision for PSE is often accorded low priority in terms of staffing and timetabling. It frequently fails to elicit a positive response from pupils or from their parents. Many schools need to review their provision and management of PSE programmes.

Many schools currently offer certification of PSE programmes at S3/S4 and S5/S6 through National Certificate modules and, in some cases, through the Standard Grade Social and Vocational Skills course. The advantages of certification are seen to include an increase in pupils' motivation and the development of a clear focus and structure for PSE which becomes part of mainstream provision. Inspection evidence indicates that certificated courses in aspects of PSE are, on the whole, successful. Non-certificated programmes vary greatly in quality between and within schools. As part of the Higher Still Development Programme it is proposed to build on the need for a coherent structure by identifying pathways for progression and certification at S5/S6.

9.   Promoting partnership

Parents have prime responsibility for their children. All guidance teams recognise this, and most have effective procedures to inform and consult parents and to enable them to enquire about any aspect of concern or interest. While most schools are reasonably successful in establishing good links with parents, there can be difficulties which need to be overcome if positive, helpful and effective communications are to be maintained with all parents. It is important that schools should be as flexible as possible in the arrangements which they make for contact with parents.

It is essential that a school's guidance policy should clearly state who is responsible for contacts between the school and parents on matters relating to guidance. There should be clear guidelines about when and how such contacts should be made, and, in the case of written communications, an indication should be given about tone and wording. There should be provision for making positive comments about pupils' achievements as well as the usual letters of concern about behaviour or progress.

To meet the needs of all pupils effectively, guidance staff will often need to supplement their own efforts by drawing on the considerable expertise of the support agencies. Most schools have satisfactory or good links with these agencies. Where there are regular contacts with careers, social work and psychological services, guidance staff usually have close links with the personnel involved, which facilitates working in partnership. However, to some extent the success of their joint efforts depends significantly on staffing stability. In several schools inspected in recent years there had been a degree of discontinuity because of changes in the organisational arrangements and personnel within the support agencies.

Links between education and the world of work have grown considerably over the last decade. The most common form of link between employers and schools is the provision of placements for work experience and work shadowing. There is also a growing diversity of arrangements which bring working people into schools to participate in seminars, team-building events, mock interviews and enterprise activities. Other schemes allow teachers to spend time in the workplace to widen their understanding of life and work in vocational contexts.

Guidance staff are also involved in establishing and maintaining links with further and higher education. For those schools where there is a history of academic achievement, the arrangements for links with higher education generally operate smoothly and efficiently. In some schools, close links have been established with further education colleges, and pupils attend college for substantial parts of their education. Appropriate arrangements are usually made for college staff to visit the school to give talks on progression opportunities and offer 'taster courses' to aid pupils' decision making. There are some schools, however, where senior management and guidance staff need to explore methods of improving the quality of links with further education colleges.

10. Management and quality assurance

Guidance provision in each school requires to be well managed and effectively co-ordinated. In a school with a good guidance system, senior promoted staff fully support the work of the guidance team. One of their number is usually assigned overall responsibility for guidance and, depending on the size of the school, is often supported by colleagues who have year/stage responsibilities. School inspections over the years have confirmed that one of the most significant factors in the management of guidance is the quality of leadership offered to the team.

Where guidance is well managed, there are clearly defined and up-to-date job descriptions for all guidance staff. Some basic elements of their remits will be common to all, but particular responsibilities and specialisms should also be identified for each member of the guidance team. Training and staff development are essential features for all guidance teachers. Senior management in consultation with guidance teachers must identify and prioritise staff development needs.

Each school should have a clear, written guidance policy drawn up with the involvement of all guidance staff. It is important, often through a guidance manual and calendar, to provide further elaboration of how the policy is implemented in practice.

Throughout the last ten years a climate of school self-evaluation has developed as a very significant feature of Scottish education. HM Inspectors of Schools have published a range of materials to assist schools conduct reviews of their own effectiveness. Education authorities have also played an important role in encouraging and developing school self-evaluation. If a school is to maintain and develop its provision of guidance, it needs to evaluate the degree to which it is successful in meeting the personal needs of pupils, and in implementing regional and national aims and policies.

Some schools make good use of the performance indicators published by HM Inspectors of Schools and/or advice and criteria established by education authorities. They adopt an appropriate balance of approaches to self-evaluation in using interviews, checklists and questionnaires, scrutinising relevant statistics (for example on attendance, referrals, or SCE performance), as well as informal discussion with colleagues as part of the review process. Some have found it particularly helpful to enlist the support of the education authority's guidance adviser. In selecting aspects to be tackled, each school should include evaluation procedures for guidance as part of the development planning process. Short and long term targets should be set as priorities within the school development plan.

1. INTRODUCTION

1.1   This report presents HM Inspectors' considered views on appropriate aims and effective provision of guidance in secondary schools. It describes and exemplifies approaches which successfully address the needs of pupils in curricular, careers and personal guidance. It is based on the evidence of over 250 inspections of guidance. The report takes account of a range of other inspection reports published by HMI including *Guidance in Dumfries & Galloway Region's Secondary Schools (1991), Aspect Report on Guidance in Four Kirkcaldy Secondary Schools (1991)* and *Careers Education in Tayside Secondary Schools (1992)*. It also draws on evidence from joint inspections with Careers Service Inspectors of careers education in schools.

1.2   Chapter 2 of the report discusses the aims of guidance and Chapter 3 describes arrangements within schools for implementing these aims. Chapters 4, 5 and 6 focus respectively on the key features of the three familiar aspects of personal, curricular and careers guidance. Chapter 7 develops the theme of personal guidance with specific reference to individual support and counselling. The contribution of education for personal and social development within a school's overall provision for guidance is described in Chapter 8. In Chapter 9, effective methods of providing and maintaining links with parents and the wider community are discussed. An overview of the management of guidance is offered in Chapter 10. Finally, the main issues and recommendations arising from the report are set out in Chapter 11.

2. HISTORICAL DEVELOPMENT, AIMS AND THE GUIDANCE PROCESS

This chapter gives a brief summary of the historical development of guidance in schools, identifies the main aims and considers the counselling process as an integral feature of effective guidance.

2.1 Teachers in Scotland have always recognised that they have a responsibility for the welfare and well-being of young people as well as for their formal academic education. There has always been help and support available for pupils, and often for their parents too, when educational decisions require to be taken, when a crisis situation arises, at school or in the home, and when important decisions have to be taken about obtaining employment or entering further or higher education.

2.2 The importance of this type of support was formally recognised by the Scottish Education Department publications *Guidance in Scottish Secondary Schools (1968)* and *The Structure of Promoted Posts in Secondary Schools in Scotland (1971)*. In the years following the publication of these documents, guidance teachers were appointed at principal teacher or assistant principal teacher level in all but the very smallest secondary schools in Scotland in a ratio of approximately one guidance teacher per 150 pupils.

2.3 In the early 1970s, systems, procedures and practices were developed gradually in individual schools across the country. By 1974, all education authorities had established guidance systems in their schools and several had appointed advisers in guidance. The latter trend was continued after local government reorganisation in 1975 as the new authorities continued to respond positively in support of schools developing their provision for guidance. In 1976, the report *Guidance in Scottish Secondary Schools: A Progress Report by HM Inspectors of Schools* indicated that the new structures had already increased the range of curricular and vocational advice and the amount of personal support given to pupils.

2.4 Over the last 20 years the notion of the school as a caring community has evolved to include the planned provision of curricular, careers and personal guidance. In *More Than Feelings Of Concern (SCCC 1986)*, the Scottish Central Committee on Guidance identified eight objectives for schools to consider. They were:

- to ensure that each pupil knows and is known personally and in some depth by at least one member of staff;

- to consider the pupils' personal, social and intellectual development;

- to help the pupil to be aware of his own development and to accept responsibility for it;

- to identify and respond quickly and appropriately to the specific needs of the individual;

- to foster the development of good relations between teachers and pupils;

- to work well with the home in all aspects of pupils' development;

- to liaise with support and welfare agencies; and

- to systematise and make effective the recording and communication of information relevant to the welfare of individual pupils.

2.5   These aims of guidance remain as relevant today as they were ten years ago. They require to be adapted to the particular circumstances of each school and expressed as unequivocal statements which underpin the philosophy of the school's concern to support the personal, social and academic development of each individual. The aims also provide the foundation on which to construct clearly stated advice on operational procedures.

2.6   The success with which guidance achieves its aims will depend on many factors, including the effectiveness of:

- support from the senior management team;

- the structures within which arrangements are made for the co-ordination and deployment of staff involved in the provision of guidance;

- the approaches adopted by staff engaged in the guidance and counselling process; and

- the links established with parents and support agencies.

All of these factors should be considered as schools review their effectiveness in achieving the aims of guidance.

Guidance and counselling

2.7   Over the last 10 years, the term 'counselling' has been increasingly associated with the process of guidance. Counselling, as it applies in schools, should not be confused with therapeutic counselling which is properly the preserve of, for example, psychologists, psychotherapists and psychiatrists. However, when individual guidance is at its most effective, it is similar in many respects to the counselling process. It is concerned with good interpersonal relationships which are based on showing respect, listening, empathising and reflecting. The development of such skills has become an integral part of all guidance staff training.

2.8   Counselling is non-directive in that it is concerned with helping pupils to reflect on their own attributes and circumstances and encouraging them to take responsibility for their own decisions. Guidance is about valuing the uniqueness of the individual and encouraging each to consider how his or her behaviour affects others. The guidance and counselling process can often involve discussion with and support for the individual who cannot meet agreed standards of behaviour and the formation of attainable goals. It involves noting and commending progress and achievements. It may demand unequivocal expressions of concern about unacceptable behaviour or lack of progress, but it should always offer strategies for dealing with these problems.

2.9   Some guidance staff make good use of counselling skills which they have developed. In the report on one school, for example, HM Inspectors noted:

> "..... a member of the guidance team with specialist experience had taken a useful initiative in providing a counselling service on an experimental basis and additionally supporting some pupils through weekly group sessions on stress management."

2.10   Most guidance staff build and sustain very good relationships with individual pupils. Many would benefit from further training in counselling skills, not to establish themselves as counsellors, but simply to assist them to develop further some of the skills which are particularly helpful in their interaction with pupils and parents.

3. GUIDANCE ARRANGEMENTS IN THE SCHOOL CONTEXT

This chapter describes provision for guidance in terms of staffing, time allocations, accommodation and resources, and analyses the effectiveness of various arrangements and structures. Within the context of guidance as a whole-school responsibility, specific reference is made to aspects of "first level" guidance and to the importance of close links between guidance and learning support.

Staffing and time allocations for guidance staff

3.1 The 1994 School Census indicates that nationally there are 1,123 principal teachers and 1,072 assistant principal teachers of guidance. In each category of promoted post, around one third of staff have a guidance-related qualification in addition to their subject qualification. Education authorities vary in their expectations concerning qualifications and training for guidance. Some expect staff to obtain a Certificate or Diploma in Guidance, and promote opportunities for them to do so. Most offer their own short 'introduction to guidance' courses, but they do not make them compulsory. Preliminary training for new appointees to guidance should be a basic requirement, followed by later opportunities for more extensive staff development.

3.2 In 1971, Circular 826 *The Structure of Promoted Posts in Secondary Schools in Scotland* allowed for the establishment of approximately one promoted post in guidance for every 150-200 pupils. Educational statistics and inspections in recent years confirm that, on the whole, this recommendation continues to be implemented across the country.

3.3 Because of the wide range in the nature and size of schools, it is not possible or desirable to lay down a uniform pattern of promoted posts in guidance or to assign specific responsibilities to these posts. The total number of guidance posts in schools can vary, not only in relation to the total roll, but also in the way in which senior management choose to deploy staff. For example, it may be that two assistant principal teachers of guidance are employed instead of one principal teacher. Such a strategy can give a broader range of options for staff deployment, more opportunities for promotion for other staff in a school, and greater breadth of experience and skills within the guidance team. On the other hand, the post of principal teacher of guidance is of importance in the school management structure, particularly in terms of team leadership. Education authorities and headteachers need to consider carefully the rationale behind the deployment of the two layers of promoted guidance posts.

3.4   In general terms, however, it is possible to state that there is appropriate provision of guidance staff where:

- the complement of guidance staff (principal teachers and assistant principal teachers) is consistently held at a level which efficiently and effectively meets the needs of the school and its pupils;

- any vacancies are filled promptly so that disruption in the provision of guidance for individual pupils is kept to a minimum;

- individual members of the guidance team have participated in relevant in-service training and staff development activities; and

- the team as a whole comprises a good blend of experience and expertise.

In addition, to avoid guidance teachers' time being eroded by administrative duties, a number of schools have arrangements in place for effective contributions from ancillary staff.

3.5   The allocation of time for guidance duties varies significantly between, and sometimes within, schools. *More Than Feelings Of Concern* did not attempt to quantify the time required to undertake the various responsibilities of guidance staff. However, reference was made to recommended allocations of 400 minutes for each guidance teacher over and above the time designated for correction and preparation. Time spent teaching personal and social education courses should only be counted as 'guidance' time in so far as it contributes to specific guidance activities within the teacher's caseload. Education authorities vary in the extent to which they advise schools about time allocations to guidance, and few authorities monitor closely the arrangements made by schools.

3.6   In one education authority, as part of a substantial policy document on guidance, some general advice is given about calculations of time for guidance staff to carry out their duties: for example, one-to-one interviews to be based on one 15 minute interview per pupil per session; time to be available for crisis counselling; one period per week to be available for a guidance staff meeting; and time spent on administrative duties also to be included in calculations. In that authority, where 400 minutes is the stated minimum recommended time for guidance duties, HM Inspectors reported that:

"..... the actual time allocations varied from school to school and from promoted post to promoted post. For example, the single principal teacher in a small school had 14 guidance periods in a 40 period week; in a much larger school, the two principal teachers each had 10 periods in a 30 period week and the four assistant principals had 12, 8, 6 and 5 periods respectively."

In another authority, in a similarly impressive policy document, advice refers to a maximum principal teacher of guidance/pupil ratio of 1/215, and a minimum 50% allocation of time to guidance for each principal teacher of guidance. Inspections of schools in that region and in other regions have indicated considerable variation in the extent to which such advice is implemented.

3.7 HM Inspectors have consistently found that the great majority of guidance staff willingly tackle a wide range of duties. In many cases guidance teachers find it very difficult to undertake these duties within the time allocated. Some become heavily involved in helping pupils with personal and social problems, some spend a lot of time on one-to-one interviews, others find involvement in careers advice very time-consuming. Sometimes, guidance teachers find that their subject teaching suffers because of the time taken with guidance matters. It is, therefore, important that guidance tasks are prioritised within a coherent attempt to manage time effectively. In some cases guidance teachers have to stand back from involvement in areas which are the responsibility of one or other of the caring agencies. Sometimes guidance staff become involved in administrative or supervisory duties that should be dealt with more appropriately by non-teaching personnel. Thus, HM Inspectors noted in one school:

> "Guidance staff knew their pupils well, particularly those experiencing difficulties, and demonstrated concern for their welfare. However, they carried a heavy workload which was likely to increase as the roll continues to rise. The school should identify the consequences of the increasing demands upon their time and look, for example, at their numbers and the use of auxiliary staff to complement their duties."

3.8 It would be inappropriate here to make specific recommendations about the priorities which must be addressed, as each school's priorities must reflect its particular circumstances. However, in general terms, schools which effectively address the problem of managing time:

- assess their priorities against the background of the community which they serve; and

- provide their guidance teams with a clear view of what is expected of them within the time available.

Accommodation and resources

3.9   The quality of accommodation allocated for guidance varies greatly between schools. Much depends on the overall range of accommodation available to each school, but an important factor is also the extent to which the school chooses to give some priority to guidance in allocating space. Some guidance teams are fortunate to have modern purpose-built accommodation at their disposal, while others strive hard to overcome the constraints of small or ageing buildings with inadequate space or limited facilities. Features of good guidance accommodation include:

- offices that are spacious, well-signposted and in a central location easily accessible to pupils, parents and staff;

- for each guidance teacher, a room or area within a team base with lockable storage facilities for records and files;

- easy access to a telephone for confidential, efficient and speedy communication internally and externally;

- a room or rooms where pupils and parents can be interviewed in privacy; and

- suitable accommodation for a careers library (usually within the school library) that is readily accessible to pupils outwith formal class time.

3.10   The majority of schools have a satisfactory range of resources to support most guidance activities. In relation to provision for elements of personal and social education, inspection evidence shows that most schools have a useful range of commercially produced materials, for example, on careers choice, drugs, health and life skills. The production of worksheets and the use of the photocopier can be time-consuming and expensive, and some schools need to monitor and review these aspects of resource provision. The use of computer technology, particularly in careers guidance, has been a significant development in the last ten years. Overall, where guidance is well resourced:

- guidance receives a favourable allocation of funds to support a wide range of activities and to develop agreed priorities;

- resources supplied centrally by the school are sufficient, appropriate, up-to-date and in good condition, for example, in relation to stationery for administration, photocopying, computing facilities and audio-visual materials; and

- the careers library is well stocked with a good range of up-to-date reference materials including information technology.

Guidance structures

3.11 In their operational structures for guidance, nearly all schools adopt 'horizontal' or 'vertical' structures, or a blend of these two basic organisational patterns. The 1988 HMI report *Management of Educational Resources: Effective Secondary Schools* identified the essential characteristics of whichever guidance structure is in place. It stated that any guidance structure will only be effective if it provides:

- appropriate information on pupils against a background of confidentiality at all times;

- sound advice and reassurance to pupils and parents, especially at times of transition from one stage to another;

- regular planned contacts with pupils and prompt responses in crises; and

- continuity of contact from year to year between each pupil and a particular guidance teacher or teachers.

3.12 Whichever structure is chosen, there are advantages and disadvantages in each. In the 'horizontal' or 'year' system, where guidance staff are responsible for age stages, some of the main **advantages** are that:

- aspects of administration and co-ordination are relatively easy to manage;

- guidance teachers' responsibilities for particular year groups can be clearly defined and easily understood by all staff;

- guidance staff have a clear focus on the features and issues pertinent to a particular year group; and

- a team approach involving guidance and other teachers is not difficult to establish as they are all dealing with pupils in the same year group.

The main **disadvantages** of the 'horizontal' system are that:

- guidance teachers' workload tends to be heavily concentrated on some specific aspects of provision;

- at particular times of the year, especially at transitions, individual guidance teachers can experience great pressure of work;

- the guidance teacher responsible for S1 pupils has a large number of new pupils to get to know;

- where pupils in different years belong to the same family, contact with the family, or with support agencies involved, is likely to be the responsibility of different guidance teachers; and

- as each guidance teacher moves up the school with the pupils, there is a gap of several years before returning through the cycle to S1 and a corresponding need for familiarisation and up-dating of expertise in particular aspects.

3.13   The main **advantages** of the 'vertical' or 'house' system are that:

- throughout their time in school, pupils from the same family can be allocated to the same guidance teacher;

- there is a manageable annual influx of new pupils for each guidance teacher to get to know;

- the workload is shared throughout the guidance team and spread more evenly throughout the year;

- guidance teachers are involved in a range of aspects of guidance each year, are better able to develop their expertise, and can gain a broader appreciation of whole-school developments; and

- a vertical system is more easily adaptable to a changing school roll.

The main **disadvantages** in the 'vertical' system are that:

- administration and co-ordination require careful management since all guidance staff are involved in all aspects of guidance; and

- it can be challenging for other teachers who may be involved in guidance to work with pupils at different stages.

3.14   It is the responsibility of individual schools to review their own circumstances and resources with a view to choosing the structure which best meets the needs of its pupils. HM Inspectors evaluate each school's guidance structure in the light of its specific circumstances and in the extent to which it meets pupils' needs. However, in the light of recent and future developments in Scottish education, the arguments in favour of a vertical structure have become more compelling.

3.15   The current implementation of the National Guidelines 5-14 is increasing the amount and quality of information about pupils entering the school in S1; and the future implementation of the Higher Still programme will pose new challenges at S5/S6. It is increasingly likely that in addressing the needs of pupils, guidance staff will find that a vertical system offers better opportunities for developing their expertise in a range of whole-school developments and a more equitable sharing of workload. Inspections have indicated that many schools were reviewing their structures in the light of such developments. The overall trend shows a movement from 'horizontal' to 'vertical' structures.

Guidance as a whole-school responsibility

3.16   The quality of guidance provision influences the tone of the whole school. It is of crucial importance in establishing and maintaining an atmosphere in which pupils know they are valued as individuals and feel encouraged to learn.

3.17   Most schools recognise that to some extent all members of staff are guidance teachers. In addition to the professional expectation that all teachers have a responsibility for addressing their pupils' educational needs, many schools explicitly state that all staff should show concern for the personal and social needs of their pupils. Subject teachers are involved in aspects of guidance when they deal with matters relating to pupil welfare and discipline in the classroom and when they use the school's referral system. Within this context, the guidance team should have a central role.

3.18   The view that guidance is a whole-school responsibility is embodied in the philosophy, concept and aims of 'first-level' guidance which have been clearly stated in *More Than Feelings Of Concern*. Whether or not schools use the term 'first-level' guidance matters little, but all schools should adhere to the idea of a whole-school approach to guidance. Briefly stated, the origins of first-level guidance lie in the relationships established through the frequent contact of pupils with particular members of staff, usually register teachers or 'tutors'. The daily pattern of contact with a register teacher, for example, provides the opportunity for a two-way flow of information on a frequency that is difficult to sustain with promoted guidance staff. However, the success of such a system depends on the commitment of register teachers or tutors to their role in the whole-school approach to guidance and pastoral care.

3.19   Some schools have specifically developed first-level guidance as part of their whole-school approach. Where it is most effective, first-level guidance staff have:

- a clear appreciation of the expectations of their role;

- the full professional support of promoted guidancestaff and opportunities for a regular interchange of information;

- individual responsibility for a group of pupils who come within the caseload of one guidance teacher;

- responsibility for the same pupil group as they progress through the school;

- significant involvement in their pupils' personal and social education programme on a voluntary basis and with full support from promoted guidance staff; and

- access to on-going school-based staff development to meet identified needs.

3.20   A particularly good example of a vertical house system enhanced by aspects of first-level guidance was seen in one school where:

"Guidance provision was effectively based on a four house system. In S1, the four promoted guidance teachers also acted as form teachers to assist them in gaining familiarity with their caseloads. In S2 and beyond, other members of staff had responsibility as form teachers for classes with whom they retained contact as the pupils moved up through the school. This strong degree of continuity effectively underpinned the house system. It also provided a good basis for first-level guidance and enhanced the social cohesion of the school."

3.21   The aims of whole school or first-level guidance are primarily pastoral, but when implemented successfully, curricular and academic aspects can be helpfully addressed. A coherent approach should help to identify personal and academic successes or difficulties at an early stage, and enable the school to respond appropriately. Effective provision of first-level guidance ensures that the staff involved contribute to aspects of monitoring, profiling and reporting on the progress of pupils for whom they have responsibility.

3.22 Clear lines of communication between guidance teachers and all other staff are essential. All staff in a school should be aware of the role of guidance teachers and should work co-operatively with them in matters which concern the pupils they teach. Guidance staff need to consult and co-operate with senior management, subject teachers, learning support staff and representatives of the caring agencies such as medical personnel, social workers and psychologists. Where communications are well-established, arrangements are in place to support regular consultation. Thus, many schools ensure that guidance teachers are available at specific times to consult with other staff: for example, prior to and during registration each day, and at designated periods when they have allocated guidance time.

3.23 Within the whole-school provision for guidance, support for adult returners is an aspect which seldom attracts sufficient attention. Adults in schools are, in general, offered some guidance support from individual subject teachers or from a member of the senior management team with this responsibility. Promoted guidance staff are rarely given a key role in adult guidance. In 1992, the HMI report *The Education of Adults* noted that over 13,000 adults were engaged in learning activities in three-quarters of the secondary schools in Scotland. The report confirmed previous findings by HM Inspectors which identified high drop-out rates among adults following courses in schools. Few schools have an effective induction programme for adults and there is little evidence of strategic planning with further education colleges. In reviewing their overall provision for guidance, schools should give more attention to the needs of adults.

Guidance and learning support

3.24 Close links with learning support staff are essential features of effective guidance arrangements. Learning support staff are usually involved with pupils across a range of subjects and have a close understanding of individual pupils' learning needs. They should therefore have strong links with guidance staff in order to address pupils' needs appropriately and consistently across the curriculum. Regular communication between the guidance team and learning support staff is an important and necessary part of the process of:

- reviewing the learning needs of pupils generally, of specific year groups, and of particular individuals;

- addressing pupils' social and academic concerns; and

- discussing referrals or potential referrals to caring agencies.

3.25   Where individual pupils have special educational needs, guidance staff should discuss with learning support staff how these needs can be met. Guidance teachers should at least be informed about communications between learning support staff and subject teachers, parents and support agencies and will often be involved in case conferences and reviews of progress of individual pupils.

3.26   Within the arrangements for transfer of pupils from primary to secondary education, guidance and learning support staff have an important role. Nearly all schools have well-established arrangements which make for a smooth transfer. Many schools ensure that information about specific learning needs is discussed jointly by learning support and guidance staff. Thereafter, it is essential that appropriate and useful information is distributed to subject teachers to assist them to cater effectively for specific needs. Many schools could improve this aspect of communication by ensuring that the information is in a form that can be easily understood and acted upon by subject teachers, and by regularly reviewing its usefulness with staff.

4. PERSONAL GUIDANCE: PASTORAL CARE

This chapter identifies the key features of personal guidance. It draws on examples of effective practice at the particularly important stage of transition between P7 and S1, and considers features of record-keeping, reporting and profiling.

Aims and objectives

4.1   All schools are concerned to maintain good relationships between pupils and teachers within a caring ethos, and most attempt to give close attention to the personal needs of individuals. For the main part, pastoral care and personal guidance are all-pervasive features of the daily contacts which teachers have with pupils. However, in certain important respects, guidance staff have a major role to play, whether that is related to their close knowledge of a particular individual's circumstances or their involvement at key transition points of a pupil's career.

4.2   A major objective for guidance staff is to ensure that they know each pupil in their case-load as well as possible. Where they have an impressive knowledge of their case-loads, some or all of the following characteristics are present:

- a guidance system that promotes good continuity of contact between pupils and their designated guidance teacher;

- a policy that ensures that each guidance teacher's remit covers the personal, curricular and vocational aspects of guidance;

- appropriate individual contacts with all pupils at least once per session;

- guidance staff involved in all key transitions (see Chapter 5);

- ready access for pupils to guidance staff and vice-versa;

- an allocation of time which takes cognisance of the size of their case-load and other designated guidance duties, approximating to 40 minutes per week for every 15 pupils for whom they have direct responsibility;

- close involvement with parents (e.g. through school reporting procedures), careers officers and personnel from other support agencies;

- regular reviews of individual pupils' progress reflected in well maintained guidance records containing a range of appropriate information;

- efficient two-way communication with other teaching colleagues which ensures effective use of information in relation to all pupils; and

- guidance staff with regular teaching commitments, including involvement in personal and social education with at least some of the pupils in their case-load.

4.3   A common aim in the job specification of guidance teachers is "to meet each pupil in the case-load at least once per year on a one-to-one basis". This is seen as fundamental in attempting not only to meet the general needs of all pupils but also to identify and address the needs which are specific to a particular pupil and which may be of a personal or confidential nature.

4.4   The extent to which guidance staff achieve the aim of one-to-one interviews for all pupils each session has often been disappointing. However, in recent years, the requirement for interviews in and beyond S3 as part of the Technical and Vocational Education, Compact or Training Credits Initiatives has improved the position. Several schools recognise the value of guidance teachers meeting small groups of three or four pupils to discuss, for example settling in to S1, or how the early part of S3 is proceeding. Such arrangements enable guidance staff to prioritise contacts with pupils who appear to require a more in-depth individual interview. The effectiveness of these small group interviews is enhanced in schools where guidance staff are timetabled to meet their own pupils each week within the personal and social education programme.

4.5   A number of schools have clearly stated aims and objectives for one-to-one interviewing as part of the guidance programme. Typically this includes a 'calendar' of when such interviews are most appropriately undertaken, for example:

- early in S1, to monitor how pupils are settling in, to emphasise the availability and approachability of guidance staff, and to ensure familiarity with the services which guidance offers;

- in the period leading to subject choice for S3 and to coincide with the issue of S2 reports to parents;

- before the end of the first term in S3 in order to monitor academic progress and to undertake some aspects of profiling;

- in S4, to discuss performance in class and in any preliminary examinations; to prepare either for subject choice for S5 or for interview(s) with the careers officer for those deciding to leave school at the statutory leaving age; and preparing relevant documentation such as references and records of achievement; and

- in S5 and S6, to prepare winter leavers for interview(s) with the careers officer; and for others to discuss performance in preliminary examinations, intentions regarding future education, applications to colleges/universities, interviews with careers officers, employers etc; and for any references or records of achievement as necessary prior to leaving school.

4.6   Within the context of pastoral care, schools have an important role to play in the specific area of protection of children. In 1990, the SOED issued Circular No 10 entitled *Protection of Children from Abuse - The Role of Education Authorities, Schools and Teachers*. The Circular advised education authorities on the arrangements they should make and the advice they should issue to their schools for identifying and dealing with suspected cases of child abuse. Abuse is defined in broad terms to cover physical injury, emotional damage and sexual abuse; it includes peer abuse and bullying. All staff, and particularly guidance staff, should be appropriately informed of the procedures to follow in relation to child protection. Many schools make good use of support packages which deal with various aspects of child protection, but there is scope for further focus on aspects of child protection in the curriculum.

P7/S1 transfer and induction

4.7   The links between primary and secondary schools and the smooth transfer from one sector to the other are essential elements in the educational process for all pupils. For the great majority of pupils the move from primary to secondary school is something that they take in their stride. Nevertheless, it should be remembered that this transition, sometimes from a small primary to a large secondary school, is likely to be the first change of school for many pupils. A well thought out transition and induction programme is therefore something that can be helpful for most pupils and reassuring for those who have real fears about the change of school. While primary and secondary schools have long recognised the value of maintaining close links, the introduction of the National Guidelines 5-14 has further emphasised the importance of continuity in pupils' experience as they move from primary to secondary education.

4.8   Guidance staff usually play an important part in these links through ensuring that the transfer of pupils is implemented smoothly. In some schools, however, there is scope for widening the extent and improving the quality of their participation in the process. The time necessary for liaison with associated primary schools must be made available and used effectively. To that effect, secondary schools require to operate a carefully structured liaison programme with clear guidance and pastoral care objectives. Effective arrangements for the transfer from primary to secondary education include some or all of the following features:

- P7 pupils meet their future guidance teacher both in the primary school and on their familiarisation visit to the receiving secondary school;

- S1 pupils contribute to liaison with their former primary school;

- P7 parents receive appropriate information and are encouraged to visit the secondary school;

- a booklet specifically written for new S1 pupils; and

- guidance staff included in discussions with primary teachers about the new S1 intake.

4.9   The ease with which guidance staff can visit primary pupils varies from school to school. Where a 'vertical' guidance system exists, with several guidance staff responsible for different groups of S1 pupils, it is not always possible to ensure that each guidance teacher meets with their own incoming pupils in the primary setting. Nevertheless, some contact should be made through a visit by a member of the guidance team or by a member of the senior management team responsible for guidance in S1. Where a 'horizontal' guidance system is in operation, with one or two guidance teachers responsible for S1, it is usually easier to arrange visits to the associated primary schools. It is recognised that there are logistical difficulties in visiting pupils in the primary setting when they come from a large number of schools within a wide catchment area.

4.10   Current S1 pupils can also contribute to the preparation for transfer by means of visits, giving talks or writing newsletters in order to help P7 pupils to form a picture of the secondary school. In one school for example:

"A number of S1 pupils visited their former primary school to speak to the P7 class about features of life in the secondary school. They had been involved in compiling an introductory video and booklet and offered personal comments on both, by way of further explanation and in response to questions from the primary pupils. Their presence in the primary school added an impressive vitality and realism to the process which was much appreciated by the P7 pupils who responded with rapt attention and pertinent enquiries."

4.11 In some schools senior pupils make valuable contributions to the transition from primary to secondary school. In one such case:

"S5 pupils, as part of their work on a National Certificate module in Communication, had completed a video recording of school life in S1. They had previously written to the associated primary schools inviting suggestions for filming and were at the stage of seeking permission to show the finished product to the P7 classes."

4.12 P7 pupils are usually introduced to the secondary school through visits to familiarise them with various features of their new school. They need to be prepared for the change of building and change in organisation and should be provided with full information about the school and the role of guidance staff. A small number of secondary schools arrange initial visits as early as October in the previous year. It is more common practice to arrange visits in June when the P7 pupils follow a sample timetable for two or three days to give them an introduction to their new surroundings and a taste of their new subjects. This sample timetable provides opportunities for the pupils to meet with their guidance teacher and their S1 register teacher or tutor. Parents too are helped in the preparation for transfer by receiving appropriate information in advance and being encouraged to visit the secondary school at a time that coincides with the P7 induction visit.

4.13 Effective liaison includes guidance staff being involved in, or made aware of, discussions with primary teachers about the new intake. These discussions, together with information from primary reports, should contribute to knowledge about individual needs. In this respect, primary schools need to be alerted in advance about the level and type of information needed by guidance staff. In gathering information two principles should be kept in mind: documentation should be brief and to the point and easily communicated to other teachers who need to be informed; and it should be capable of substantiation, not based on hearsay or unsupported opinion. Further comment on guidance teachers' awareness of particular individuals' needs is made in Chapter 7.

4.14 Most education authorities offer advice to schools on various aspects of the organisation and delivery of guidance. The following basic checklist of activities for transition and induction at P7/S1 draws on the advice contained in one such education authority guidance manual:

In preparing for a visit to a primary school, guidance staff should:

- arrange the date, time, place and duration of visit;

- tell the school who will be visiting;

- identify the aims and purpose of the visit;

- identify specific information that is requested about pupils;

- ask the primary school to:

    - brief their pupils about the nature of the visit
    - tell the pupils the name(s) of the visiting guidance teacher(s)
    - invite their pupils to suggest things they want to know about and inform the secondary school of the responses received
    - ensure that all reports are completed;

- prepare answers to queries raised by primary pupils;

- prepare a list of subjects which pupils will study in S1; and

- have a simple map of the secondary school.

During and after a visit to a primary school, the following questions should be considered:

- are there groups of pupils who should be kept together or separated?

- are there pupils with special educational needs, recorded or not?

- are there pupils with exceptional talents or abilities?

- to whom and how is the information to be disseminated?

- should particular parents be contacted before their children come to the school?

4.15 Effective personal guidance is characterised by a systematic monitoring of the way the new entrants settle in to the school. It is essential that guidance staff are aware of how S1 pupils are adapting to the new school organisation and structure, to new courses and different approaches to teaching and learning, and to making new friendships. In the vast majority of schools, guidance staff are well aware of pupils who are having particular difficulties in settling in and take appropriate action to assist them. Most schools ensure that all S1 pupils are interviewed individually or in groups during the first term, and some have established systematic procedures for gathering information from subject teachers about how well each individual is adapting to new surroundings and experiences. Good practice has been seen in some schools where this information is transmitted to parents before the end of the first term.

4.16 In one school, for example, HM Inspectors noted that:

> "A major strength of pastoral care early in the secondary school included provision for a 'guidance clinic' in November. Information about individual S1 pupils was gathered from subject teachers and collated systematically by guidance staff for a meeting with parents to inform them of how their children were settling in at school. The guidance clinic, the work of guidance and learning support staff, and a recently introduced behaviour incentive scheme were very positive features of personal guidance."

4.17 It is particularly important that guidance staff quickly demonstrate their concern to get to know **all** pupils. Schools have a range of strategies to maximise the level of contact between guidance staff and their S1 pupils; two common ones have already been identified, viz., close involvement of guidance staff at the P7 stage and individual/small group interviews early in S1. A growing number of schools timetable guidance staff to teach the personal and social education programme for S1 pupils in their case-load. In others, emphasis is placed on timetabling some of the guidance teachers' S1 subject teaching to be with pupils in their case-load. In a few schools, guidance staff act as S1 register teachers for the first month or so in order to meet pupils at least once per day. A small number of schools provide short residential visits for each S1 class with their register and guidance teachers.

4.18 Nearly all schools recognise that an essential part of helping pupils to adjust to new surroundings lies in monitoring aspects of attendance, taking appropriate action over absenteeism and explaining expectations about behaviour. Guidance staff are usually very closely involved in monitoring attendance, often through their links with register or first-level guidance teachers. Many guidance staff take the view that the identification of attendance problems early in a pupil's secondary career often prevents, or at least delays, an escalation into serious truancy or other deviant behaviour patterns. Even in S1, guidance teachers spend a considerable amount of time on matters relating to the attendance of particular pupils.

4.19 In recent years, guidance staff in most schools have developed more appropriate roles in relation to their involvement in matters of discipline. Their role in disciplinary procedures is more typically that of counselling and support to complement the application of sanctions. In S1 it is important that the roles of register teacher/first level guidance teacher and guidance staff are clarified. It is also important that these staff display consistent attitudes towards disciplinary and referral systems for all pupils throughout S1 to S6. Over the last few years, the majority of schools have reviewed their disciplinary systems realising that their caring image would be compromised if 'pastoral' staff were too closely associated with the imposition of sanctions.

4.20 Overall, inspection evidence indicates that schools give high priority to pastoral care arrangements at P7/S1, and into S1. A significant investment of guidance staff time is felt to be justified in order to gain the early confidence of pupils; and to signal to parents which member of the guidance team has particular responsibility for the care of their children. The following extract from a report on an exceptionally effective guidance department offers an example of high quality provision.

> "Guidance teachers made a valuable contribution to the transfer of pupils from the associated primary schools to the secondary school. They interviewed each P7 pupil individually, focusing on the pupil's record of achievement in the primary school. During a two-day visit to the school in early June, pupils followed a sample timetable which included a period of personal and social education with their guidance teacher. Later in the month, guidance staff took part in a sports day for all of the incoming pupils; senior pupils helped to organise this event. The school had also organised workshops, held in the associated primary schools, to raise parental awareness of its personal and social education programme. It also held an information evening for S1 parents in October to describe and explain the curriculum their children were undertaking."

Record-keeping, reporting and profiling

4.21 In meeting the needs of all pupils, guidance teachers require to maintain accurate and up-to-date pupil records; they must also ensure the proper security of these documents or databases and appropriate access to such records. All staff should be familiar with the provisions of the School Pupil Records (Scotland) Regulations 1990 and, in relation to information held on computer, with the *Data Protection Act 1984.* Normal practice in the majority of Scottish schools is for guidance staff to have responsibility for the Pupil Progress Records (PPRs) and for these records to be stored securely in the guidance office(s). Guidance teachers usually keep copies of all communications including reports, notes of interviews and phone calls etc. in the relevant PPR. Such a system can avoid the worst excesses of guidance staff keeping their own records separate both from the PPRs and from any other system that senior promoted staff may operate. Most schools have appropriate methods of monitoring records, but some guidance teachers need to be more meticulous in recording contacts with pupils and parents.

4.22 For many years guidance staff have maintained a profile of information designed to assist in the development of a rounded picture of each pupil's academic progress and attainment, social competence, vocational inclinations and interests. Such profile records are invaluable to staff: when completing references and assisting pupils with their applications for jobs or for entry to courses at college or university; for briefing careers officers or other support agency personnel; and for reporting back to parents. In recent sessions guidance staff in many schools have become involved in various aspects of producing a National Record of Achievement (NRA). The main purposes for the formal recording of achievements are:

- so that the learning and experience gained by each individual can be recognised and credited by the individuals themselves, teachers, parents, supervisors, training managers, careers officers and employers;

- to motivate and aid personal development so that individuals can more easily recognise and evaluate their own achievements, consider opportunities available, and plan for the future;

- to help review learning and other experiences and to stimulate good approaches to teaching, training and learning so that all parties can work to ensure that the opportunities available match the needs of the individual; and

- to provide, for those leaving school or making any other transition, a useful portfolio of evidence and an informative summary of their achievements which can also be used as a basis for further development.

5. CURRICULAR GUIDANCE

This chapter identifies the key features of effective curricular guidance. It draws on examples of effective practice at important stages of transition (e.g. at S2/S3 and S4/S5). The role of guidance staff in the transition from P7 to S1 has been outlined in Chapter 4.

5.1   Guidance has a central role in ensuring that all young people achieve their academic potential during secondary education. Effective monitoring of pupils' progress is a basic pre-requisite in creating a situation where guidance staff can assist pupils and their parents at, for example, important transition stages when choice of subjects or courses of study have to be made. Key stages for the monitoring of academic performance are: the early phases of S1, S3, and S5; as part of preparation for subject choice in S2 and S4; and around the period of 'prelims' for external examinations. Inspection evidence shows that schools are not consistently effective in monitoring progress; a significant number of schools require to give more attention to this important aspect of guidance, particularly beyond S2.

In S1 and S2

5.2   In most schools there are satisfactory arrangements for liaison between guidance and subject staff in reviewing pupils' progress in S1 and S2. The importance of close links between guidance and learning support staff has been particularly significant in schools experiencing an increase in the numbers of pupils who have special educational needs and who may also have Records of Needs. Most guidance staff collate progress reports from their subject colleagues and make constructive comments on school reports to parents and to pupils themselves. Inspection reports show that in the great majority of schools, monitoring of progress in S1 is recognised as particularly valuable in assuring both pupils and parents that the transition from primary to secondary education had been satisfactorily achieved. In most schools, pupils' expected and actual progress are reviewed appropriately throughout S1 and S2; some schools, however, require to give more attention to monitoring progress, particularly in S2.

5.3   Individuals who are not performing to expectations are usually interviewed by guidance staff so that action towards realistic targets can be negotiated and agreed. Some schools take appropriate steps to ensure that the monitoring process includes pupils whose progress and/or effort deserves commendation. Such practice, and the encouragement of self-referral by pupils (and their parents) to discuss progress at any time in these early years, helps to project a positive image of guidance. There remains, however, a significant number of schools where guidance is associated only with pupils who are experiencing difficulties; these schools should give more attention to recognising the attitudes and effort of individual pupils across the range of abilities.

5.4 Some schools encourage pupils to assess their own progress and aptitudes and to contribute to the preparation and maintenance of personal profiles. In one school, HM Inspectors noted that:

> "The school had made significant progress in introducing regular self-assessment. Commendably, pupils were involved throughout their school career in updating their National Record of Achievement. They learned to be aware of the skills they were acquiring, assess their abilities and record their achievements in an appropriate manner."

Where guidance staff are closely involved in monitoring progress and also responsible for maintaining pupil progress records and/or profiles, they are easily able to provide an up-to-date and comprehensive briefing or profile on any pupil for whom they have a specific responsibility.

Transition from S2

5.5 The transition from S2 to S3 is a very important stage in a pupil's career and is recognised as such in all schools. During S2, schools prepare pupils for the choice of those subjects or courses which they hope to follow at subsequent stages. Guidance staff should be in a strong position to advise and assist them to make appropriate subject choices. If they know their pupils well, they can offer informed advice, taking account of personal characteristics, preferences, aspirations and parental wishes in the context of national recommendations on breadth and balance in the curriculum at S3/S4.

5.6 The preparation for, and implementation of, arrangements for S2 choice of courses for S3/S4 is a period of intense activity for guidance staff and pupils. In nearly all schools guidance staff are at the centre of the process through which pupils come to make decisions about their preferred options. Guidance teachers require to be aware of subject departments' reports on individuals' progress, indications of future potential, and the nature of available courses and teaching groups. While the emphasis at this stage lies in ensuring that pupils keep their options open through continuing with a broad and balanced curriculum, they also have to consider the implications of pupils' decisions on future careers. To achieve the desired aim of placing every pupil on a suitable course, within the constraints of the timetable, guidance staff need an appropriate allocation of time and resources.

5.7 Effective provision for the transition from S2 to S3 includes the following characteristics:

- a carefully planned programme of events to assist pupils prepare for option choice;

- specific responsibility for the programme and its implementation invested in a member of the guidance or senior management team;

- at least one opportunity for all S2 pupils to discuss their course choice with their guidance teacher;

- a structured teaching programme, usually within the personal and social education course, with activities and experiences designed to help pupils to make sensible, informed and realistic decisions and choices;

- opportunities for pupils to consider the implications of particular choices as they relate to future careers through discussion with staff, systematic introduction to the school's careers library, and access to information made available by the school's careers officer; and

- encouragement to pupils to talk about their options with parents, both before and after a special S2 parents evening on the topic of course choice for S3/S4.

5.8 Familiarisation with the careers library should enable pupils to develop skills in retrieving information and in accessing sources of ideas about careers. Particularly useful arrangements include:

- provision of a simple booklet to familiarise pupils with the main facilities of the careers library;

- arrangements for the careers officer and guidance staff to offer S2 pupils practical experience in using the careers library;

- opportunities for S2 pupils to use the careers library at lunch or after school.

At this stage some schools successfully introduce pupils to simple computerised careers information packages. There is, however, a significant minority of schools where pupils either have no formal introduction to the careers library or where the facility itself is of poor quality.

5.9   At all stages in the process before final course choices are made, it is common to find evidence of wide consultation between guidance staff, subject teachers, pupils, parents and careers officers. For various reasons schools accept the need to make changes to some individual pupils' choices after the planned process has been completed. Requests for changes sometimes come from the pupils and/or their parents; sometimes they are made on the advice of subject teachers. Most guidance teachers satisfactorily explain the necessity for any change to the pupil and parents and ensure that it meets with their agreement. When alternative choices are offered, most guidance staff take appropriate account of any effects on pupils' career aspirations.

5.10   All schools recognise the importance of keeping parents informed of the option choice principles and procedures, and invite them to meetings to discuss their children's choices of S3 subjects. A number of schools promote the joint attendance of parents and pupils at the S2 parents' evenings; parents and pupils usually welcome the opportunity and careers officers are usually in attendance. In view of the importance of decisions taken at this time, it is a practice with considerable benefits to all concerned.

5.11   Many schools hold two meetings, the first of which serves the purpose of informing parents about the structure of the curriculum in S3/S4 and advising them of national expectations of breadth and balance across the modes of learning. At that meeting senior management or guidance staff invariably emphasise the key role played by each pupil's guidance teacher and invite parents to indicate any questions or concerns that they have. The second meeting is usually held prior to the final decision on choice of course and gives an opportunity for parents to discuss progress and options with subject teachers, guidance staff and careers officers. Commendably, some schools evaluate the success of meetings with parents by seeking their views on questions such as the extent to which they were satisfied with the arrangements and with the coverage of relevant issues, and invite them to suggest improvements.

5.12   Most schools produce useful booklets to convey information and offer advice to both pupils and parents about choosing courses at the end of S2. In many parts of the country these are helpfully complemented by information produced by the careers service. The standard of school produced booklets is generally good, but in a number of schools closer editing of booklets is required to achieve a greater consistency in the style of contributions across subjects.

Transition : adapting to S3

5.13   Monitoring pupils' progress early in S3 is a key feature in good guidance practice. Guidance staff, on the whole, appropriately identify and follow up reports on pupils whose performance is causing concern to subject teachers. Many schools, however, need to monitor more closely the performance of **all** pupils across their curriculum. In the relatively small number of schools where this is done effectively, guidance teams have established impressive arrangements for monitoring systematically the progress of all pupils in their new courses. Good practice includes the systematic collation of information about all pupils from subject teachers and learning support staff. Such information helps guidance staff to ascertain which pupils are:

- requiring further help beyond that available within subject departments;

- underachieving simply because they are not applying themselves; and

- making particularly good progress which deserves recognition.

The third of these points re-affirms the importance of promoting a positive image of guidance. As indicated in paragraph 5.3 above, in too many schools the emphasis on identifying poor performance reinforces the notion that guidance staff work only with 'problem' pupils, and contributes to the rather negative image that many parents, pupils and other staff have of guidance provision. It is essential to recognise the efforts of those pupils who have made genuine improvements in performance and/or attitudes. All too often, inspections reveal that letters to parents relate solely to difficulties which pupils are experiencing.

5.14 The full potential of one-to-one follow-up between a guidance teacher and pupil is best realised when guidance staff adopt a forward-looking, target-setting approach to reports rather than simply offer a retrospective summary. It is still quite rare to find guidance staff monitoring the outcomes of their curricular advice to individual pupils. Guidance teachers are ideally placed to monitor pupils' progress across the curriculum in a holistic manner. The need for systematic liaison and co-operation between guidance staff and subject teachers is again stressed as a crucial component in identifying and addressing particular pupils' needs.

Transition from S4 into S5 and S6

5.15 The transition to the upper school, particularly the move from S4 into S5, has assumed greater importance as a period requiring a special guidance focus. In recent sessions schools have been faced with both an increase in numbers of pupils staying on beyond S4 and a greater diversity of academic abilities and interests in S5 and S6. Inspection evidence shows that the preparation for option choice in S4/S5 frequently fails to meet the quality of provision in S2. There are often only limited opportunities for pupils to discuss their options with their guidance teacher and, in a significant number of schools, the contribution of guidance staff to S4/S5 option choice procedures is minimal. In some schools this contrasts sharply with the good practice of close involvement of guidance staff at the S2/S3 stage; often it is senior promoted staff rather than guidance teachers who provide the main input with individual pupils in S4 to S6.

5.16 Overall, the expectations already noted with regard to the extent and quality of provision in S2 also apply in S4. Thus, the interaction between guidance staff, subject teachers, pupils, parents and careers officers, should continue to be given close attention at S4, with an obvious shift in emphasis towards implications for the post-school phase of pupils' careers.

Transition: adapting to S5 and S6

5.17 Increasingly, guidance staff are involved in monitoring the progress and attainment of pupils in the upper school years as they approach national examinations. This is particularly important because pupils' plans for the future frequently depend on success in these examinations. At this stage, effective guidance continues to be founded on systematic liaison with subject teachers to ensure that pupils' expected and actual progress are compared at regular intervals. Anomalies, again usually on the negative side, are generally followed up appropriately by interviews with the pupils concerned and with parents if necessary. While pupils at all stages and their parents should be encouraged to contact guidance staff to discuss any matters of concern, it is particularly important that at the upper stages early action is taken to help with any difficulties.

Some implications of Higher Still developments

5.18 The successful implementation of the Higher Still development programme will require high quality guidance for all pupils. Support currently provided by schools will, in future, need to be adjusted to meet the needs of pupils following Higher Still programmes.

5.19 Good quality curricular guidance will be very important in ensuring that the new arrangements and greatly increased range of opportunities work to the advantage of all pupils. At S4, S5 and S6, systems and procedures will need to be reviewed to assist pupils in making sensible choices and to monitor their progress along their chosen pathways.

5.20 In relation to curricular guidance, the following issues will require to be addressed.

- Guidance teachers and pupils will need to have a wide range of current information in order to choose appropriate programmes of study which are coherent, have sufficient breadth and offer clear progression routes. This includes information about units, courses, group awards levels, entry and exit points, vocational opportunities and the implications of the various choices available.

- Some guidance teachers will require additional staff development and training opportunities.

- Guidance staff will have a major role in monitoring pupils' progress across programmes, in the core skills and in self-review. In addition, the guidance process should provide a supportive context within which core skills can be refined and developed.

6.   CAREERS GUIDANCE

In reviewing how schools assist pupils to prepare for their future after they leave school, this Chapter describes current provision and indicates important features of good practice.

6.1   All pupils need to prepare for their future after they leave school. This preparation involves them in clarifying their ideas about the range of opportunities open to them in further and higher education, training and employment. They need assistance to make well-informed and realistic decisions based on their knowledge of themselves and of the opportunities available. Careers education is therefore an essential part of guidance provision. Careers-related activities should be planned within a clear rationale to provide a progressive and coherent experience for all pupils as they progress through secondary education. In partnership with the Careers Service, guidance staff in nearly all schools are closely involved in the design and implementation of the careers component of personal and social education programmes.

6.2   Schools have different patterns of providing careers-related activities. In some, careers education forms an important part of timetabled personal and social education programmes throughout S1 to S6; in many, there are timetabled inserts at the S2-S4 stages; in a few, there is no regular timetabled provision and any input is achieved by extracting pupils from mainstream subject classes. Inspections indicate that the most successful approaches to careers education are found in schools where responsibility for delivering and monitoring the quality of provision is clearly identified; and where senior management and guidance staff co-operate closely to ensure that the various elements of careers education are effectively co-ordinated. Inspection evidence also indicates that pupils respond best where they have experienced careers education as part of their normal curriculum.

6.3   Most schools give little emphasis to careers education at the S1 stage; appropriately, they give increasing attention to this aspect as the pupils move through the school. Some, however, have established the beginnings of a personal profile which contain early thoughts about future employment linked to self-assessment, awareness of interests, and identification of personal strengths and weaknesses. In S2, virtually all schools provide identifiable elements of careers education and guidance in the processes leading up to curriculum choice for S3 and S4. The usual pattern of provision has been identified in Chapter 5.

6.4   In S3 and S4, progressively more attention is given to broadening the pupils' awareness of the range of opportunities open to them in higher education, further education, training and employment. Many schools use a computerised interest inventory as part of their provision in S3 or S4. Most need to take more account of the fact that effective use of such computer programs requires sufficient time to examine and analyse the reasons for the various suggestions in individual print-outs. Nearly all schools arrange for pupils in S4 and beyond to attend careers conventions and open days, and to hear speakers on various aspects of industry, commerce and the professions.

6.5 In S4, work experience is an important feature for all pupils and is increasingly being integrated within the personal and social education curriculum. Essential features to be addressed include the appropriate matching of pupils to placements, thorough preparation for the experience, and planned opportunities for the pupils to consider and discuss what they have gained from the exercise. In most schools the personal and social education programme in S4 and beyond reflects the importance of job-seeking skills. The most frequent topics are the completion of curricula vitae, employment/college applications, the development of interview skills (sometimes involving local employers in 'mock-interview' situations), and further work on self-assessment and the value of the careers library.

6.6 Some of the major contributions from careers officers have traditionally occurred towards the end of S3 and throughout S4. Normally there are talks and presentations outlining the role of the careers service and introducing pupils to the principles of careers choice. The practice of careers officers interviewing a large number of individuals during the S4 stage is changing as a result of the higher staying-on rates in and beyond S5; there is now more demand for interviews with careers officers from pupils in S5 and S6.

6.7 It is important that guidance staff provide appropriate briefing information for careers officers about a week prior to their interviews with pupils. Inspections have revealed that in some cases guidance teachers should be more meticulous in addressing this requirement. Interviews with careers officers are all the more worthwhile where pupils have also been prepared for and briefed about the purposes and outcomes that they could realistically expect of the interview. Only a relatively small number of schools consistently provide this type of preparation.

6.8 The majority of schools now ensure that pupils and parents are appropriately informed about courses, employment, training opportunities and the requisite qualifications for each. Many prepare and distribute useful information packs about available options. However, only a few provide helpful printed advice on financial matters such as how to apply for the available grants, loans and bursaries; or on legal aspects of employment, taxation and national insurance. Guidance staff are not always as well informed as they should be on the various opportunities that are open to school leavers.

6.9   At S5 and S6, the range of careers-related activities normally entails further use of computerised and printed careers information packages, opportunities to attend careers conventions, college and university open days and to hear speakers on various aspects of the world of work. Further opportunities are often provided for senior pupils to participate in work experience; at this stage some schools offer work shadowing as a more appropriate means of gaining first-hand evidence of a wider range of occupations and professions.

6.10   In many schools, careers education is enhanced by a range of schools-industry liaison activities. Pupils benefit from an introduction to the world of work through direct contact with representatives of industry and through participation in activities which simulate real-life contexts for decision-making, problem-solving and negotiating. Senior pupils often find 'understanding industry' courses to be enjoyable and worthwhile. Sometimes, in the context of preparation for work experience, schools simulate the employment market by establishing realistic 'job shops' and requiring pupils to apply for placements in which they are interested. Participation in 'Young Enterprise' activities also gives pupils some useful insights into the world of work. In all of these contexts it is important to ensure that issues such as equal opportunities and gender stereotyping are effectively addressed.

6.11   In one school where careers education was of high quality, HM Inspectors commented:

> "Careers education was a strength. Activities in S1/S2 included an introduction to the well-organised careers library, contact with the careers officer, use of appropriate computer programs, and attendance at an equal opportunities conference. S3 pupils had a good understanding of how to pursue interests in possible careers and were aware of the vocational importance of particular courses. From S3 to S6, pupils had a rich variety of opportunities to extend their understanding of the world of work. Work experience was very well organised by a senior teacher; tutors visited pupils on placements. Pupils were well briefed in advance and their experiences were discussed and evaluated on completion of the placement."

6.12   A well-resourced, regularly up-dated and easily accessible careers library is essential. It is usually best located within the main school library. In many schools responsibility for the facilities rests with the school librarian whose presence generally ensures that the resources are used to good effect. A member of the guidance team should liaise regularly with the librarian and careers officer. Good practice in some schools involves senior pupil in routine maintenance and daily oversight of the careers information resources.

6.13　In some schools a member of staff, usually from within the guidance team, is identified as the 'careers specialist'. Their remit is often to co-ordinate careers-related activities and to liaise with careers officers in the planning and implementation of their work. This arrangement has advantages for the school, the Careers Service and the pupils. It is important, however, that these specialists are members of the guidance team and do not operate in isolation from mainstream guidance activities. It is also advisable that expertise is shared with other members of the team so that coverage and continuity can be preserved during staff turnover or absence.

6.14　A commendable development in recent years has been the drawing up of service level agreements between schools and careers services. Representatives of both parties to the agreement meet to review what has been achieved in the previous year and plan for the range of activities for the following year. Agreement is reached on the volume of activity and the respective roles of guidance staff and careers officers in achieving the agreed objectives.

7. PERSONAL GUIDANCE: INDIVIDUAL SUPPORT AND COUNSELLING

This Chapter concerns the important role for guidance staff in offering support to individual pupils who have particular learning and/or behaviour difficulties, or are attempting to cope with personal crises or decisions. It also takes account of the very particular needs that certain pupils have in resolving problems associated with curriculum and careers issues.

7.1 In meeting individual needs, guidance staff recognise that personal 'crisis' points sometimes occur with little warning or time for preparation (e.g. family bereavements); others arise within the normal pattern of school life (e.g. transition points, examination periods). The length of time over which a pupil requires specific support and counselling can be relatively short or encompass the whole of secondary education. Nearly all guidance staff appropriately recognise that when the need is specific to a particular individual, issues of confidentiality are involved.

Individual pastoral care

7.2 As previously indicated, the essential characteristic of effective guidance is that each pupil knows and is known personally and in some depth by a member of the guidance team. While guidance staff do not always have in-depth knowledge of some of the quiet, well-adjusted pupils on their caseload, most are very familiar with the circumstances of pupils who present difficulties in terms of behaviour, attendance, and under-achievement.

7.3 All schools claim that a high priority for guidance staff is the identification of particular needs of individual pupils. This is certainly one of the key objectives of guidance programmes relating to transition points such as P7/S1 and subject/course choice. Individual needs are identified in various other ways, for example through monitoring academic progress, attendance and discipline referrals, or in the preparation of reports to parents. Important information is brought to the attention of guidance staff by parents and outside agency personnel. Sometimes individual pupils or their friends communicate concerns to guidance staff.

7.4 The extent to which pupils take the initiative in seeking the help of guidance teachers is an important indicator of the effectiveness of guidance provision in a school and of the confidence which pupils have in their guidance teachers. Some schools have successfully encouraged self-referral. For example, in one school:

> "Pupils were strongly encouraged to contact their guidance teachers, and staff were reassured by the fact that a number of pupils took up this option. There was evidence of a satisfactory response to self-referral and also of guidance staff initiatives to encourage pupils to seek support from other members of staff."

7.5   Guidance staff can find that much of their allocated time is spent in supporting a small minority of their caseload. Inspections indicate that, in some schools, the following aspects absorb much of the guidance resources available:

- matters relating to truancy, including school refusal;

- aspects of family breakdown, bereavement, and social deprivation issues such as long-term unemployment;

- behaviour problems based on inability to cope with school discipline procedures and/or the manner of their application;

- difficulties over personal relationships, for example bullying, personal safety, teenage/adolescent sexual behaviour (contraception, teenage pregnancy, homo-sexuality);

- significant under-achievement in relation to academic potential, particularly when due to inappropriate teaching in relation to the most able pupils and those with marked learning difficulties;

- problems relating to unexpected failure in external examinations; and

- medical/health problems (e.g., substance abuse, stress, the onset of serious illness, handicap).

In dealing with these aspects of their work, guidance staff need to call on many of the counselling skills previously identified in paragraphs 2.7 to 2.10.

Learning and behaviour support

7.6   Recent inspection evidence indicates a welcome increase in the extent and quality of co-operation between guidance staff and teachers involved in the provision of learning and behaviour support (including that for pupils with special educational needs, whether recorded or not). In one school, for example, HM Inspectors reported:

> "The school had established a joint team of teachers and staff from a range of support agencies to discuss the most appropriate provision for pupils with behavioural and other problems. This group decided on possible strategies which were then offered to relevant staff within the school."

Discussions involving guidance and learning and behaviour support staff frequently address the very specific pastoral and social needs of pupils whose difficulties are considerable; and who, until fairly recently, may not have been in mainstream education. The unique and complex nature of particular individuals' needs is posing new challenges for guidance staff.

7.7   Successful integration of pupils with special educational needs requires a high degree of teamwork between guidance and learning support staff. A small number of schools have established the practice of timetabling a period so that the relevant guidance and special educational needs teachers can meet to review progress and plan ahead on a weekly basis. Such an arrangement has been particularly successful in meeting exceptional needs and in enabling specific children to maximise their integration or re-integration within mainstream.

7.8   There is value in guidance staff retaining teaching commitments and being directly involved in encouraging and maintaining the disciplinary code of the school in and beyond the classroom. As promoted members of staff they have a particular contribution to make; this contribution will be shaped and informed by their assigned responsibilities for knowing the pupils in their charge. As a point of reference for pupils and staff, and as a person with whom problems can be discussed, the guidance teacher is in a unique position: to help individual pupils to cope with any difficulties they may be experiencing in school; to recognise early warning signals in pupils' patterns of conduct; and to take appropriate action which may prevent or forestall instances of indiscipline.

7.9   On the basis of the relationships which have developed and their knowledge of pupils and their circumstances, guidance teachers are able to intervene effectively when evidence begins to emerge of a deterioration in pupils' attitudes, behaviour or relationships. Guidance staff have a vital role to play:

- in counselling individual pupils and parents before behavioural problems become intractable;

- in giving support when things go wrong;

- in liaising with other professional groups with an interest in the pupil; and

- in providing advice, support and feedback to all teaching colleagues.

Support for individuals: curriculum and careers

7.10 Individual support on all aspects of curricular and careers guidance is a major dimension of guidance provision during secondary education. The range of need is extensive. For example, at the early stages pupils and parents may wish to discuss career aspirations in general; with senior pupils, very specific advice and information may be sought concerning the next steps to be taken in entering employment or post-school education.

7.11 During S1 and S2, an important aspect of individual support focuses on the choice of subjects to study during S3 and S4. For most pupils, the degree of support given in the personal and social education programme and through one-to one interviews with guidance staff is appropriate. For some individuals, more discussions with guidance staff and/or subject teachers are required in order to resolve particular issues. Frequently in such situations close contact with parents complements work with pupils, particularly over questions of achieving a balanced course which ensures as wide a range of future careers as possible. In a very small number of cases the support of the visiting careers officer is enlisted in order to provide the pupil and/or parent with further independent advice.

7.12 Beyond S1 and S2, guidance staff are often involved in responding to complex demands associated with curricular and vocational issues for particular individuals. These usually involve co-operation with subject teachers, senior staff and parents; the vocational implications of specific advice often involve the careers officer. Inspections have indicated that the extent of this aspect of guidance work with individual pupils is increasing as more pupils, representing an ever-widening range of ability, opt to stay on at the S5 and S6 stages.

7.13 The typical whole-school provision of careers education and guidance has already been indicated in Chapter 5. There are many points when individuals wish to focus on their own career and employment prospects. At these times, pupils frequently engage the support of a wide range of people including family, friends, subject teachers, careers officers, guidance staff, and liaison personnel from post-school institutions. There are several ways in which guidance staff assist individual pupils over careers issues. These include advice in relation to option choices at the end of S2 and S4, answers to specific queries arising from careers literature, and involvement in the preparation and debriefing activities associated with effective work experience and work shadowing schemes.

7.14   Individual support and counselling on careers matters increases steadily as pupils progress through secondary education, reaching a peak as final decisions and plans are made about the post-school phase of life. Most schools appropriately support individual pupils over applications for jobs, in the provision of references, in preparation for specific interviews relating to employment or to post-school education, and over entry procedures for colleges and universities.

8.   EDUCATION FOR PERSONAL AND SOCIAL DEVELOPMENT

This chapter identifies appropriate aims in education for personal and social development and reviews the quality of provision of personal and social education (PSE) programmes.

Rationale and aims

8.1   Education for personal and social development has long been recognised as an important aspect of the work of schools. *Curriculum Design for the Secondary Stages (SCCC 1989)* noted that ".... society expects aspects of personal and social development to appear within the school curriculum" and identified key elements of personal and social development. *The Structure and Balance of the Curriculum 5-14 (SOED 1993)* states:

> "..... the whole curriculum should contribute to the personal and social development of pupils. They will learn to identify, review and appraise the values which they and society hold and to recognise that these affect thoughts and actions. They will take increasing responsibility for their own lives, will develop a positive regard for others and their needs and will be able to participate effectively in society. The achievement of these aims requires pupils to increase their knowledge and understanding about themselves, others, their immediate environment and the wider world. They will also need to develop skills which will enable them to care for their personal needs; to assess their own capabilities; to work independently and with others; and to make decisions."

These aims apply not only to pupils in the 5 to 14 age range. They are, without exception, applicable to 14 to 18 year olds.

8.2   In recent years, national debate on key aspects of the education of young people has emphasised the importance of the 'core skills' of communication, numeracy, personal and interpersonal skills, problem solving and information technology. Drawing on the increased recognition of these important skills and abilities, recent advice within the Higher Still Development Programme indicates that the development of core skills is a priority. The Higher Still consultation document *Core Skills* states:

> "The reason for the growing significance attached to the development of these core skills lies in the changing nature of society. Social and occupational structures are changing rapidly and this recognition has led to an emphasis on those

broad skills and abilities which are of value in a wide range of contexts in work and other aspects of life. In a rapidly changing world, competence in the core skills is essential as a foundation for lifelong personal development."

8.3   Education for personal and social development must therefore include the core skills. Specific programmes in personal and social education (PSE) should have important contributions to make, particularly in the aspects of communication, problem solving and personal and interpersonal skills.

8.4   The rationale for the *National Guidelines for Personal and Social Development 5-14* commences with the clear and unequivocal statement that "Personal and social development is a fundamental aspect of the education of the whole child." The aims are to help pupils to:

- have an appropriately positive regard for self, and for others and their needs;

- develop life skills to enable them to participate effectively and safely in society;

- identify, review and evaluate the values they and society hold and recognise that these affect thoughts and actions; and

- take increasing responsibility for their own lives.

8.5   In 1995, *The Heart of the Matter* was published as a discussion paper based on a review of personal and social education conducted jointly by the Scottish CCC and the SOED. This document recognises the imperative of providing young people with:

"a sound foundation on which to base moral and ethical decisions and behaviour which respect the dignity of themselves and others and the nature of the inter-dependent world in which we live".

The paper takes the view that:

"there are qualities or dispositions which are generally acknowledged as fundamental to any recognisable form of moral life, as a sound guide on which to base personal choice and as central to the prospering of a just and democratic society. They are:

- respect and caring for self
- respect and caring for others
- a sense of social responsibility
- a commitment to learning
- a sense of belonging."

8.6   In education for personal and social development therefore, pupils should be encouraged to increase their knowledge and understanding about themselves, others, their immediate environment and the world in which they live. They need to learn and practise processes and skills which will enable them to:

- look after their personal needs;

- work independently;

- participate effectively in groups;

- make their own decisions; and

- assess their own capabilities.

8.7   Clearly, responsibility for implementing these aims cannot, and should not, reside entirely with guidance staff. In planning effective education for personal and social development, schools must consider the implications of the whole school, cross-curricular and special focus approaches advocated in the National Guidelines 5-14. Education for personal and social development is therefore a whole-school responsibility. It contributes to and derives from a positive, caring ethos in which pupils feel supported. It takes place through the formal curriculum because all school subjects have aims relating to personal and social development. It also takes place through the informal curriculum where, for example, the quality of relationships among and between staff and pupils and involvement in extra-curricular activities contribute significantly to pupils' personal and social development.

8.8   There are particular aspects of personal and social development which are most effectively promoted through specific PSE programmes. These could include selections from within the range of SEB short courses in health studies or SCOTVEC modules in various aspects of personal development; planned programmes related to education-industry links, activities and experiences; SEB Standard Grade courses in Social and Vocational Skills; and special focus programmes in PSE.

8.9   Inspection evidence indicates that the importance of PSE prog-rammes is not reflected in a consistent quality of provision in schools. There is good practice in some schools, but overall, standards are too variable. PSE is often accorded low priority in terms of staffing and timetabling. It frequently fails to elicit a positive response from pupils or from their parents. Teachers need to apply the same standards and rigour in PSE as they do in teaching their own specialist subjects. There is, therefore, a need for many schools to review and improve their provision of PSE.

PSE programmes: quality of courses

8.10 Advice on the content and skills to be developed in PSE programmes is available from a wide range of sources. Above all, PSE programmes should focus on the development needs of pupils at the various stages of the school. *The National Guidelines for Personal and Social Development 5-14* indicate desired outcomes that are fundamental to PSE. The National Guidelines emphasise the development of concepts and skills related to self-awareness, self-esteem, inter-personal relationships, and independence and interdependence. These are seen to be key areas within which schools are encouraged to focus on specific content and skills; and they apply beyond the S1/S2 stage in secondary schools.

8.11 Typically, PSE courses cover aspects of careers education, health, and values/relationships which are addressed progressively as the pupils move up through the school. As indicated above, the courses should contribute significantly to the development of core skills.

8.12 Most importantly, courses in PSE should be relevant to the needs and interests of pupils at specific stages of their school life. Furthermore, to make a positive impact, the courses must be seen by the pupils to be relevant to their circumstances and experience. These factors have been given greater priority in various reviews and improvements to the content of PSE programmes in recent years. Well-constructed courses exhibit the following characteristics:

- the contexts and purposes of activities relate appropriately to pupils' lifestyles, social circumstances and aspirations;

- there is a broad and balanced programme which receives well-judged time allocations with appropriate emphasis given to constituent elements;

- the sequencing and pacing of the programme take due account of pupils' abilities and levels of maturity; and

- parents are informed about the nature of programmes and are made aware of approaches to controversial issues such as aspects of sex education and the misuse of drugs.

PSE programmes: quality of teaching, learning and assessment

8.13 With reference to teaching approaches and learning activities, effective PSE programmes typically provide opportunities for pupils to consider, discuss and review their experiences. Active, pupil-centred learning approaches are adopted, often using group activities, to encourage pupils to become increasingly independent and able to take responsible decisions in a wide range of contexts.

8.14 In schools where teaching approaches are particularly effective, the aims of PSE are shared with pupils who are clear about the purposes of activities and what they are expected to achieve. A range of teaching strategies and resources are used to address the aims of the course and good interaction between teachers and pupils underpins learning.

8.15 The following list offers an indication of what constitutes effective learning and teaching in PSE.

- Teachers have established a learning environment which encourages pupils to produce work of high quality. Praise is used regularly to motivate pupils who work well and enthusiastically without close supervision.

- Pupils are developing confidence in a range of skills. They have opportunities to work independently and to co-operate with others. They are developing their abilities to contribute their own ideas and to respond to conflicting viewpoints in decision-making situations. They are encouraged to reflect critically on ideas presented to them.

- Pupils have the opportunity to reflect on their own personal development and review their progress. Teachers support pupils in realistic self-assessment and target-setting activities.

- Pupils have opportunities to develop their awareness of social norms and expectations, and to reflect on these in the light of their own values. They are developing an understanding and respect for social and cultural differences.

- Particularly at S4 and beyond, pupils are consulted about the content of special programmes and activities.

8.16 Most schools give appropriate attention to assessment and recording pupils' progress across the range of subjects in the curriculum; few schools, however, give similar consideration to assessment and reporting in PSE. In this respect, good practice can be described as follows.

- Individual pupil progress and development is discussed regularly with pupils, parents and staff. All are kept informed in such a way that they can support adjustments to provision for individuals.

- There is an effective system for monitoring individual pupil progress and development which allows for appropriate adjustment to planned courses and activities in PSE.

- Well-conceived arrangements for record keeping provide for brief but perceptive comments; regulations concerning confidentiality and access to records are scrupulously observed.

- Pupil self-evaluation is encouraged as a constituent element of profiling and negotiation of targets contributes to the compilation of records of achievement.

- Deliberate efforts are made by staff to gain feedback from pupils and parents; the information acquired is used appropriately to adjust the school's approach to PSE.

PSE programmes: management issues

8.17   In many respects the management of PSE programmes requires the same focus of attention as the management of any other area of the curriculum. There should be, for example, brief but informative position statements on aims, learning and teaching approaches, resources and staff development. However, there are some features of the management of PSE that require specific attention because of the nature of the timetable arrangements, content or methodology.

8.18   The support and commitment of senior promoted staff are essential to the effective delivery of PSE programmes. Overall responsibility for co-ordinating the provision of PSE should normally rest with a member of the senior management team or with a promoted guidance teacher. Management issues that require careful planning, monitoring and review include:

- regular communication among PSE teachers and with other staff to ensure coherence in the delivery of the PSE programme throughout the school;

- contacts with associated primary schools to promote a common approach to PSE in line with the National Guidelines 5-14;

- contacts with outside agencies (e.g. careers service personnel) who contribute to the PSE programme;

- regular review and evaluation of whole school provision for PSE;

- identification, prioritisation and provision of staff development support and in-service training.

8.19 In one school where the provision of PSE was particularly impressive, HM Inspectors commented:

> "The principal teacher of guidance who had responsibility for PSE had developed a very good programme from S1 to S6. The courses covered a range of appropriate themes using well-chosen resources. On sensitive topics, parents' views were sought. The attempts by staff to link pupil activities to their own experience and future needs were rewarded by willing participation and signs of growing self-confidence. Response to the programme was monitored and changes made as necessary. Commendably, senior pupils were consulted on topics for their course. There were 14 staff involved in PSE: they were chosen for their strengths in interacting with pupils, and had benefited from well-targeted in-service training."

Progression and certification in PSE

8.20 The issues of progression and certification in PSE have been the subject of some debate in recent years. *The National Guidelines on Personal and Social Development 5-14* set out a framework by which progression may be described. The document recognises that

> ".....when assessing pupils' personal and social development, progression should not be regarded as linear; personal rates of development are not and cannot be standardised".

However, within a broad framework for progression, it is possible within a coherent whole school PSE programme to focus on various ways in which pupils develop knowledge, understanding, attitudes and skills.

8.21 Many schools currently offer certification of PSE programmes at S3/S4 and S5/S6 through National Certificate modules and, in some cases, through the Standard Grade Social and Vocational Skills course. The advantages of certification are seen to include an increase in pupils' motivation and the development of a clear focus and structure for PSE which becomes part of mainstream provision. Inspection evidence indicates that certificated courses in aspects of PSE are, on the whole, successful. Non-certificated programmes vary greatly in quality between and within schools. As part of the Higher Still development programme it is proposed to build on the need for a coherent structure by identifying pathways for progression and certification at S5/S6.

9. PROMOTING PARTNERSHIP

This Chapter identifies important ways in which guidance contributes to the quality of the partnership which schools have with parents, support agencies, employers and post-school education.

Links with parents

9.1   Parents have prime responsibility for their children. All guidance teams recognise this, and most have effective procedures to inform and consult parents and to enable them to enquire about any aspect of concern or interest. These procedures cover pupil reports, parents' meetings, individual interviews, letters and telephone calls and a range of documents, such as prospectuses and newsletters.

9.2   If a close partnership with parents is to be achieved, it is necessary in the first instance to communicate clearly the purposes, activities, opportunities and support available through guidance. In brief, good school handbooks for parents:

- provide clear statements about the centrality of guidance to effective learning and personal development;

- give full information about the guidance-related services which are available both in school and outside; and

- identify ways in which parents can contact the school and whom they should contact in the first instance.

9.3   There are numerous reasons for, and benefits from, establishing regular contacts between school and parents. All schools offer opportunities for parents to meet in a range of school-based contexts. For parents the advantages include getting to know the layout of the school, becoming acquainted with individual staff members and senior management, and meeting among themselves for informal discussion and sharing of information. Exceptionally, and usually for very specific reasons, home visits by guidance staff have proved helpful.

9.4   While most schools are reasonably successful in establishing good links with parents, there can be difficulties which need to be overcome if positive, helpful and effective communications are to be maintained with all parents. Most guidance staff are appropriately sensitive to the fact that some parents feel uneasy or nervous when dealing with the school, and try to create a relaxed and non-threatening atmosphere in their parental contacts. Guidance staff sometimes complain that the parents they most want to see are the ones who do not turn up to parents' evenings. It is therefore necessary for schools to look at ways in which this unsatisfactory situation can be improved rather than by accepting it as inevitable. Parents may fail to attend meetings for various reasons which have nothing to do with an unwillingness to visit the school. It is, therefore, important that schools should be as flexible as possible in the arrangements which they make for contact with parents. In one education authority's guidance policy manual it is recommended that where considerable distances are involved for parents travelling to meetings, the associated primary schools could be used as alternative venues.

9.5 It is essential that a school's guidance policy should clearly state who is responsible for contacts between the school and parents on matters relating to guidance. There should be clear guidelines about when and how such contacts should be made, and, in the case of written communications, an indication should be given about tone and wording. Inspection evidence indicates that most schools have established appropriate policies, but that several, which rely heavily on standard letters to cover a range of circumstances, should review the content of these letters which can be, variously, very impersonal, condescending, patronising or negative and censorious in tone. It is important that the emphasis in contacts between guidance staff and parents should focus on positive aspects rather than simply on the occasions when problems have arisen. Thus, there should be provision for making positive comments about pupils' achievements as well as the usual letters of concern about behaviour or progress.

9.6 The following points are offered as checklists of good practice:

(i) In relation to meetings with parents:

- every effort is made by school staff to create a welcoming and friendly atmosphere, whether for a large meeting of parents or for individual consultation;

- adequate direction and other relevant instructions are clearly displayed so that visiting parents can clearly identify key locations of, for example, the school office, senior management and guidance staff;

- interviews are conducted in private and, as far as possible, without interruption;

- interviews are held in surroundings which are as comfortable and inviting as possible;

- guidance staff who have been given responsibility for addressing meetings of parents are properly briefed as to the purpose and intended outcome of the meetings; and

- guidance staff are flexible in their approach to meetings or interviews, and, where possible, make arrangements to suit parents who are unable to attend on particular occasions.

(ii) In relation to letters and telephone calls:

- letters to parents may be of a standard form agreed by the school's senior management team; the tone and content of these letters are, however, closely scrutinised to ensure that they are appropriate to the particular circumstances of each pupil;

- individual letters are sent only by members of staff designated by the headteacher;

- copies of all letters sent are kept on file;

- letters dealing with particularly sensitive matters are signed by the headteacher, or are at least authorised by him before being issued;

- all letters are followed up until a satisfactory response is achieved; and

- records are kept of telephone calls to and from parents.

9.7   *More Than Feelings of Concern* devoted a separate chapter to "Guidance and the Home" because of the fundamental importance of the issues raised in the relationship of home and school. There is evidence that in recent years schools in general and guidance staff in particular have been increasingly aware of the need for a genuine partnership with parents. A good example was seen in the inspection of guidance in four secondary schools in one town. HM Inspectors reported:

"All schools attached great importance to developing close relations with the parents of their pupils. Guidance staff participated in, and contributed to, many of the meetings with groups of parents held for various reasons and had responsibility for making contact with parents by letter or telephone when information had to be exchanged. There was evidence to suggest that, overall, guidance staff had achieved very satisfactory relations with parents, sometimes in difficult circumstances and that they had gained the confidence of most parents with whom they had been in touch."

Links with support agencies

9.8 To meet the needs of all pupils effectively, guidance staff will often need to supplement their own efforts by drawing on the considerable expertise of the support agencies. In addition to the Careers Service (Chapter 6), the main focus of liaison is usually with the Psychological Service and the Social Work Department, but links with the Health Service and Children's Panels are also important. The help of these services is invaluable, not only for pupil referrals, but also for expert help and advice on a consultancy basis.

9.9 Guidance staff have the responsibility of ensuring that the services provided to the school are delivered effectively. There are, therefore, details relating to administration and communication that must be clarified for the benefit of all involved. Schools which have the most effective arrangements for liaison and co-operation with the support agencies include their representatives as part of the extended guidance team and encourage the development of an ethos within which the contribution of these agencies is highly valued. Reporting on one such school, HM Inspectors commented:

> "Within the extended guidance team, the exchange of information among key staff including the attendance officers and school-based social worker was a particular strength. Brief, but prompt and informative feedback to subject departments on referrals was appreciated. Guidance staff and the school-based social worker worked closely together in dealing with a wide range of referrals, sometimes in the demanding role of advocate for the pupils concerned. They co-operated effectively on specific initiatives such as group work designed to improve pupils' behaviour".

9.10 Key features of effective liaison with support agencies include:

- policies within which arrangements for communication and co-operation with the support services and referral procedures are clearly stated;

- regular meetings (at least once per term) between guidance staff and representatives of the support services; and

- the identification of individual guidance teachers who have specific responsibilities for liaison with named personnel in each of the support services.

9.11   Most schools have satisfactory or good links with the support agencies. Where there are regular contacts with social work or psychological services, guidance staff usually have close links with the personnel involved, which makes it easier for them to work in partnership.   However, to some extent the success of their joint efforts depends significantly on staffing stability. In several schools inspected in recent years there had been a degree of discontinuity because of changes in the organisational arrangements and personnel within the support agencies.

9.12   There are often important issues of confidentiality resulting from liaison with support agencies. In many schools there is scope for better communication of information to subject teachers, particularly where such information is relevant to a pupil's performance in classwork or to their health and safety. Guidance staff and agency personnel generally need to give more attention to discussing the content of information that should be communicated to other staff within the normal bounds of confidentiality.

Links with employers and other agencies

9.13   Links between education and the world of work have grown considerably over the last decade.   TVEI has influenced the curriculum significantly and has made a major impact on education-industry links (EIL). The TVEI requirement that pupils have direct contact with employers, for example through work experience, has acted as a catalyst for the changes advocated in other national developments such as the Standard Grade and National Certificate programmes.   The process of contacting employers to arrange work experience places has led to other valuable interactions between schools and industry.   These include pupil visits to industry and industrial inputs to the school curriculum, to careers education and to the personal development of pupils through activities such as mock interviews.

9.14   There are many examples of good practice in the area of EIL, and pupil reaction to these initiatives is generally favourable. Guidance staff, TVEI co-ordinators, schools' EIL co-ordinators, careers officers and Schools Industry Liaison Officers employed by education authorities have contributed much to improved awareness of the world of work. Most recently, education business partnerships (EBPs) have begun to play a key role and some schools have taken full advantage of the opportunities which they provide. Pupils benefit from the wide range of collaborative activities which include representatives from business and industry visiting schools and first hand experience of short periods in the workplace.   The establishment of the Compacts initiative in areas of deprivation has enabled schools involved in these arrangements to enter into more extensive partnership agreements with employers. Guidance staff have been centrally involved in the Compact agreements on, for example, attendance targets and job and training pledges.

9.15   The most common form of link between employers and schools is the provision of placements for work experience and work shadowing (both usually of one week duration).   There is also a growing diversity of arrangements which bring working people into schools to participate in seminars, team-building events, mock interviews, and enterprise activities. The Teacher Placement Service has been a substantial influence in enabling teachers to spend time in the workplace to widen their understanding of life and work in vocational contexts.   As far as S5 and S6 are concerned, the most important arrangements are those which give access to work experience and work shadowing and the opportunities to join with business people in workshop events to explore the nature of business and industry.

9.16   Where EIL is effectively managed, guidance staff make significant contributions to the arrangements.   Pupils are prepared for their work experience during PSE time and have extensive debriefing with their guidance teacher.   HM Inspectors commented on good practice seen in one school where:

> "Pupils were given the responsibility of organising their own placement, from initial contact with the provider to the final report on their experience. This was adjudged by these pupils to be the single most important event in the development of their personal skills and responsibility in school."

Links with further and higher education.

9.17   Guidance staff are also involved in establishing and maintaining links with further and higher education. For those schools where there is a history of academic achievement, the arrangements for links with higher education generally operate smoothly and efficiently.   Pupils are encouraged to go to Open Days and often arrange such visits themselves. In most cases, guidance staff provide appropriate information in advance, and comprehensive, up-to-date information on degree and diploma courses is available in the careers library.

9.18   In some schools, close links have been established with further education colleges and pupils attend college for substantial parts of their education. Appropriate arrangements are usually made for college staff to visit the school to give talks on progression opportunities and offer 'taster courses' to aid pupils' decision making. There are cases, however, where senior management and guidance staff in schools should explore methods of improving the quality of links with further education colleges.

10. MANAGEMENT AND QUALITY ASSURANCE

This Chapter reviews the main priorities for effective management of guidance. It outlines key features in managing staff, accommodation and resources and identifies the importance of establishing clear policies and procedures for quality assurance.

10.1 The resource pack *Managing Guidance,* published by SOED/Northern College/St Andrew's College in 1994, provides schools with a great deal of useful information, advice and exemplars to assist in the process of reviewing and evaluating the quality of management of guidance. Within the four broad headings of 'Guidance Documentation', 'Managing a Guidance Entitlement', 'The Image of Guidance' and 'Managing First Level Guidance', this substantial pack is intended to support and facilitate the effective management of guidance. It provides a useful tool for focusing on some of the key features and issues identified in this and other chapters.

Management of staff

10.2 In order to meet the complex, numerous and wide-ranging needs of pupils, guidance provision in each school needs to be well managed and effectively co-ordinated. In a school with a good system of guidance, senior promoted staff fully support the work of the guidance team. One of their number is usually assigned overall responsibility for guidance and, depending on the size of the school, is often supported by assistant headteachers who have year/stage responsibilities. School inspections over the years have confirmed that one of the most significant factors in the management of guidance is the quality of leadership offered to the team. Effective leadership of guidance is seen where the guidance co-ordinator ensures that:

- everyone in the team knows what is expected of them;

- there is full consultation on all guidance issues;

- he/she sets a professional example which motivates staff to give of their best and which contributes to a good team spirit among the guidance teachers;

- there are regular meetings of the guidance team; and

- there are good communications with senior management and other staff.

10.3 Where guidance is well managed, there are clearly defined job descriptions for all guidance staff. Some basic elements of their remits will be common to all, but particular responsibilities and specialisms should also be identified for each member of the guidance team. Thus, appropriate remits identify the involvement of guidance staff with pupils, indicate the nature and frequency of the contact to be maintained, specify the approaches to liaison with parents, colleagues and external agencies, and outline the main responsibilities in respect of record-keeping.

10.4 The deployment of guidance staff needs careful consideration to ensure that pupils' needs are catered for as effectively as possible in each school. Within the constraints imposed by rapid changes in roll or staffing, guidance teachers and non-teaching staff are deployed appropriately when:

- pupils remain with the same guidance teacher throughout S1 to S6;

- it is easy for subject teachers to know which guidance teacher to contact for a referral;

- guidance teachers' remits provide for a balanced coverage of the major guidance functions;

- remits also provide for specialisation within the team; thus, individual guidance teachers may be assigned responsibilities for specific aspects such as liaison with primary schools, learning support, careers education, or personal and social education, etc; and

- the duties of non-teaching staff are clearly defined: for example, office staff are clear about their role in taking messages and making appointments, the librarian has specific responsibilities covering some aspects of use of the careers library.

In addition, there should be appropriate distinctions between the responsibilities of principal teachers and assistant principal teachers.

10.5 Thoughtful management of staff also ensures that guidance cover is available for most of the school day. More schools should adopt the good practice of drawing up a duty roster to show times when individual members of the guidance team are available for informal or formal consultation or appointments; and publicising the availability of staff to pupils, parents and outside agencies. At the same time, it is important that the class teaching commitments of each guidance teacher are accorded appropriate priority, free from casual interruption whether caused by pupils, other staff or parents.

10.6 Since the formal introduction of guidance in the late 1960s there have been many wide-ranging developments in secondary education. Training and staff development are therefore essential features for all guidance teachers. Senior management in consultation with guidance teachers must identify and prioritise staff development needs. Decisions about staff development priorities should be based on the needs and interests of the school as a whole and of each individual guidance teacher, taking account of the balance of skills and expertise within the guidance team. School development plans which are well-conceived include guidance-related staff development activities, drawing on expertise within the school and using opportunities provided regionally and nationally. In schools which effectively address the need for staff development in guidance, all members of the guidance team are likely to have attended in-service courses within the last five years and/or participated in a sustained school-based staff development programme. Overall, guidance teachers should have access to a wide range of short in-service courses as well as longer courses which lead to a qualification at certificate or diploma level.

10.7 Inspections have revealed that most education authorities make satisfactory or good provision for staff development in guidance. In one authority, for example, HM Inspectors reported in 1991:

> "A strategy for in-service training provided a firm indication of the region's commitment to improve and reinforce the quality of guidance. It comprised five main strands. First, courses of four weeks duration leading to the award of a Certificate in Guidance, were arranged in conjunction with a college of education; more than 50 teachers had attended these courses over the past three years. Second, training was offered in the use of computers for aspects of careers guidance; this training, available to all guidance staff, unpromoted teachers and careers officers, attracted a large response. Third, a series of five 3-day courses to enhance counselling skills was mounted, to which representatives from the Careers Service, Psychological Services and Community Education were also invited. Fourth, training courses on combating the misuse of drugs were provided to members of extended guidance teams. Finally, a special one-day course on AIDS successfully attracted representatives from the Schools Councils, the pre-cursors to School Boards."

In this education authority it was a rare occurrence to find a member of a school's guidance team who had not attended some form of training. Indeed, the majority of guidance teachers had taken part in several courses.

Management of accommodation and resources

10.8 In guidance, as in all other aspects of the work of a school, good management of the available accommodation and facilities is essential. Where these aspects are effectively managed, senior management and the guidance team ensure that, for example, the guidance base or guidance teachers' rooms are attractive and welcoming, and that interview rooms offer privacy and are appropriately furnished. Most guidance teams are meticulous in making sure that records and confidential information are kept under lock and key.

10.9 In most schools, resources for guidance are satisfactorily managed, but there is scope for more attention being given to this aspect of management. It is not uncommon, for example, to find that individual guidance teachers hold useful materials in their own offices that should be disseminated for information or for use by other staff. In the best cases:

- there is a well-planned whole-school approach to allocating funds to the various aspects of guidance;

- books, materials and equipment are catalogued and well-organised in a central location, easily accessible to teachers and pupils;

- very good use is made of the range of guidance and whole-school resources, including the careers library and information technology; and

- the guidance team regularly review the use of resources, check that they are up-to-date, and make informed decisions about resource needs and priorities.

Policies

10.10 Senior management teams give crucial support by becoming intimately involved in the formulation of aims and in the preparation of specific policies covering the wide range of guidance activities. Within the senior management team, the task of the headteacher, or more commonly the depute or assistant headteacher to whom responsibility for guidance has been assigned, is to ensure that policies are translated into practice by specifying objectives and priorities and laying down operational guidelines.

10.11 Each school should have a clear, written guidance policy drawn up with the involvement of all guidance staff. When all staff in a school are fully consulted in the formulation or review of guidance policy, and where there is a genuine sense of ownership of, and commitment to, the policy, there is a good chance that it will be implemented effectively across the school.

10.12 A school's guidance policy statement need not be lengthy. It should identify clearly and succinctly:

- the aims and purposes of guidance;

- the way guidance is organised in the school;

- the services provided by the guidance system;

- the services available through the guidance system; and

- the remits of guidance staff.

These points should be included in the relatively brief statement of guidance policy. They should be expressed in clear terms in the school prospectus, booklets for new pupils and their parents, and in the internal staff handbook. The wider readership of School Boards, parent-teacher associations and support agencies should also be considered.

10.13 In recent years HM Inspectors have noted improvements in the quality of the documentation which underpins guidance provision. In one school where aims, policies and procedures had been carefully formulated, HM Inspectors recorded:

> "The school handbook listed eight aims for guidance staff, the first of which appropriately identified the importance of knowing and being known by the pupils in their care. The excellent guidance handbook clearly identified remits, calendars of events for each year group and operational procedures."

10.14 As indicated in that extract, it is also necessary to provide further elaboration in, for example, a guidance manual of how the policy is implemented in practice. The manual should provide details on the functions of guidance and advice on all aspects of the school's arrangements for guidance. These are likely to include provision for partnership with parents and support agencies, confidentiality, record keeping, links with subject departments, arrangements for referrals, and approaches to timetabled programmes of personal and social education.

10.15 A guidance calendar is a very useful feature of most schools' guidance documentation. It serves the important function of informing all staff of the annual pattern of guidance activities; and acts as a diary to remind guidance teachers of dates for initiating or responding to the annual cycle of whole-school or year group guidance activities. The following headings (with dates and deadlines appropriate to each school) are typically included in guidance calendars:

S1 visits to associated primary schools
   visits to secondary school by primary pupils
   reception of new intake
   check primary progress reports; disseminate information
   pupil interviews
   profiling/NRA activities
   preliminary/final reports to parents
   parents' evening

S2 pupil interviews
   profiling/NRA activities
   course choices S2 into S3
   reports to parents
   parents' evening (particular reference to course choices)
   course alterations

S3 pupil interviews
   profiling/NRA activities
   monitor progress/problems in new courses
   careers information
   reports to parents
   parents' evening

S4 pupil interviews
   profiling/NRA activities
   careers information/interviews
   SCE presentation checks
   16+ induction, option form
   transition from school to FE, employment, etc.
   reports to parents
   parents' evening
   emergency consultation post SCE

S5/6 pupil interviews
   profiling/NRA activities
   advice on study skills/decision making
   monitor progress/problems in 16+ courses
   UCAS applications

visits from FE/HE personnel
SCE presentation check
university/college open days
reports to parents
parents' evening

Quality assurance

10.16 Throughout the last ten years a climate of school self-evaluation has developed as a very significant feature of Scottish education. HM Inspectors of Schools have published a range of materials to assist schools conduct reviews of their own effectiveness. Education authorities have also played an important role in encouraging and developing school self-evaluation. If a school is to maintain and develop its provision of guidance, it needs to evaluate the degree to which it is successful in meeting the individual needs of pupils, and in implementing regional and national aims and policies.

10.17 In achieving effective self-evaluation, senior management must be sensitive to the need to establish a positive climate within which all staff are encouraged to engage in the processes of review. In all approaches to self-evaluation, every effort should be made to ensure that:

- the aims of evaluation are clearly understood by all involved;

- evaluation is seen as a positive, non-threatening aid to progress, with the identification of positive features and strengths as well as the acknowledgement of weaknesses forming the foundations for development;

- the whole exercise is manageable;

- it leads to decisions about future priorities, to manageable targets, and to strategies for improving provision;

- it is accurate and unbiased; and

- the results are open to scrutiny.

With specific reference to guidance, it is important to establish the position where self-evaluation is seen as a natural part of the ongoing work of the guidance team.

10.18 Some schools make good use of the performance indicators published by HM Inspectors of Schools and/or advice and criteria established by education authorities. They adopt an appropriate balance of approaches to self-evaluation in using interviews, checklists and questionnaires, scrutinising relevant statistics (for example on attendance, referrals, or SCE performance), as well as informal discussion with colleagues as part of the review process. Some have found it particularly helpful to enlist the support of the education authority's guidance adviser. In one school, for example:

> ".....an evaluation of guidance provision by an outside consultant had been sensibly used to guide further monitoring."

Several schools have found it beneficial to seek the views of all parties involved - pupils, parents, staff and support agencies.

10.19 There are many features of guidance that lend themselves to self-evaluation. The following list of questions is by no means exhaustive, but gives an indication of aspects worthy of review.

(i) <u>The impact of guidance on school ethos</u>

To what extent does guidance contribute in encouraging staff and pupils to identify with the school's aims and ethos?

To what extent does guidance improve pupils' levels of motivation and achievement?

How positive are pupils' attitudes to school in general and to guidance services in particular?

How well does guidance contribute to the quality of relationships, levels of respect and co-operation among and between staff and pupils?

How effectively has guidance influenced the views of parents and the local community about the school? (For example, do parents visit or communicate with the school for positive reasons rather than because of problems?)

(ii) <u>Building relationships and personal support</u>

How effective are the arrangements to ensure that each pupil knows and is known by at least one member of the guidance team?

Is the best possible provision made for continuity in pastoral care?

What is the extent of, and what are the main reasons for, referrals (including self-referrals) of pupils to guidance staff?

Are the pupils' levels of self-awareness, self-esteem and self-confidence appropriate?

How well do pupils respond to individual contacts and interviews with guidance staff?

How accurate and up-to-date are pupil records?

(iii) Curricular guidance and careers advice

How effectively does guidance help pupils to make important transitions?

To what extent are pupils satisfied with their choices of subject at transition points?

How well do pupils adapt to new subjects and different teaching and learning approaches?

How effectively does guidance help pupils make choices of careers, post-school education and training?

How effective is the level of co-operation between guidance staff and Careers Service personnel?

(iv) Personal and social education

How well does the personal and social education programme fulfil its aims and objectives for all pupils across the range of abilities?

What are the views of pupils, parents and staff on the programme?

Within the personal and social education programme, to what extent are pupils actively involved in their own learning, and how far does the content reflect the needs and interests of pupils?

(v) Liaison

To what extent are staff in the school familiar with the functions of guidance, and what are their attitudes to guidance?

How good are the relationships between guidance staff and other school staff, pupils, parents and support agencies?

How effective is the system of referrals to guidance from teachers, parents and support agencies, and how successful are the outcomes of referrals?

(vi) <u>Management issues</u>

How effectively is the school implementing regional and national policies on guidance?

How clear is the school's policy statement on guidance and how useful (to guidance teachers and to other staff) is the related documentation?

To what extent are guidance staff involved in management decisions and policy formulation?

What level of priority is given to guidance by senior management?

How effective are communications between senior management and guidance staff?

What is the quality of teamwork and relationships among guidance teachers?

How effective are guidance team meetings?

10.20 Schools which are concerned to maintain and improve the quality of guidance engage in formal and informal aspects of self-evaluation as an ongoing feature of their work. Guidance encompasses such a wide range of activities that senior management teams and guidance staff have to prioritise areas for particular focus over a period of time. In selecting aspects to be tackled, each school should include evaluation procedures for guidance as part of the development planning process. Short and long term targets should be set as priorities within the school development plan.

10.21 While every feature of guidance provision should be kept under review, the level of staff expertise in the various functions of guidance should be closely considered within the development planning process. Opportunities for in-service training and staff development across the whole range of guidance activities are essential for all guidance teachers; they should also be available to other teachers who, for example, contribute to aspects of first level guidance or help to teach elements of personal and social education. Within the numerous areas in which in-service training and staff development can help teachers improve their expertise and professionalism, inspections indicate that priorities to consider include the development of:

- skills in counselling, negotiating and interviewing;

- knowledge of provision at 16+, particularly with the advent of the Higher Still programme;

- knowledge and skills in first level guidance activities;

- expertise in profiling, assessment and recording; and

- familiarity with information technology.

10.22 Where the management of guidance is effective, senior promoted staff and the guidance team are committed to evaluating and developing the guidance system using indicators of performance as described in this report. In one such school HM Inspectors reported:

> "Strong leadership, good personal relationships at all levels, and an energetic and enthusiastic guidance staff who regularly reviewed the quality of their work, were major factors in the success of the day-to-day operation of the guidance system in the school. A secure and caring environment had been created in which, almost without exception, the daily problems arising in a large and varied community were dealt with quietly, sensitively and effectively. There was ample evidence to suggest that, for the great majority of pupils, school was a happy experience."

In that school the senior promoted team and guidance staff liaised closely to ensure guidance provision was efficiently and effectively managed. The extract offers an indication of the very significant influence of a well-managed guidance system on the overall tone, ethos and atmosphere of a school.

11. ISSUES AND RECOMMENDATIONS

A series of issues has been raised in this report. This Chapter identifies those of highest priority and makes recommendations to those concerned with the future development of guidance.

Guidance arrangements in the school context

11.1   Because of the wide national range in the nature and size of schools, it is not possible or desirable to lay down a uniform pattern of promoted posts in guidance or to assign specific responsibilities to these posts. However, education authorities and schools have the responsibility of ensuring efficient and effective patterns of provision.

- **Education authorities and headteachers should consider carefully the needs of each school in relation to the staffing of guidance. For example, there should be a clear rationale in the remits and deployment of assistant principal teachers and principal teachers (3.3, 3.4).**

11.2   Guidance staff undertake a wide range of duties. Time management is an important issue that must be addressed.

- **Headteachers and guidance staff should assess their priorities against the background of the communities which they serve. Guidance staff should have a clear understanding of what is expected of them within the time available. Education authorities should monitor the extent to which guidance staff are able to provide an effective service within their allocation of 'guidance' time (3.5 - 3.8).**

11.3   Guidance structures should reflect the most effective way of meeting the needs of pupils. The report describes some advantages and disadvantages of horizontal and vertical guidance structures.

- **Senior management and guidance staff should review their guidance structures in the light of arguments expressed in this report (3.11 - 3.15).**

11.4   The quality of guidance provision influences the tone of the whole school. Many schools recognise that to some extent all teachers are guidance teachers. Each school's aims of and approaches to guidance should be clear to all staff.

- Senior management and guidance staff should ensure that the responsibilities of all staff and the specific remits of guidance teachers are clearly understood; and that there are well-defined lines of communication between guidance teachers and all other staff (3.16 - 3.22).

11.5 Close links between guidance and learning support staff are essential features of effective guidance.

- Senior management should ensure that guidance and learning support staff liaise effectively in addressing pupils' needs (3.24 - 3.26; 7.6 - 7.9).

Personal guidance: pastoral care

11.6 A major objective for all guidance staff is to ensure that they know each pupil in their case-load as well as possible. In particular, guidance staff have an important pastoral role in the transfer of pupils from P7 to S1. Chapter 4 offers a number of indications of good practice in this aspect of guidance.

- Senior management and guidance staff should establish arrangements and procedures which facilitate regular contact between guidance teachers and the pupils in their case-load (4.1 - 4.5).

- Senior management should ensure that guidance teachers are closely involved in the arrangements for the transfer of pupils from P7 to S1. Guidance staff should give high priority to monitoring how well S1 pupils are settling in (4.7 - 4.20).

Curricular guidance

11.7 In most schools, guidance staff are effective in monitoring the progress of pupils who are experiencing difficulties. In many schools, there is a need to give more attention to monitoring the progress of all pupils across the range of abilities.

- Guidance staff should review their approaches to monitoring the academic progress of pupils in order that good progress is recognised as consistently as poor performance (5.3, 5.13)..

11.8 Most guidance staff are appropriately and effectively involved in helping S2 pupils prepare for option choice. They are often less involved or less effective in assisting pupils in S4, S5 and S6 to make choices about subjects or post-school education or employment.

- **Senior management and guidance staff should review and evaluate the provision of curricular guidance for senior pupils (5.15, 5.16).**

- **Close consideration should be given to the implications of the Higher Still development programme (5.18 - 5.20).**

Careers guidance

11.9 Careers education and careers-related activities are essential features of effective guidance.

- **Senior management and guidance staff should review and evaluate the provision of the various elements of careers education to ensure that pupils benefit from a coherent whole-school approach (6.1, 6.2).**

11.10 Computer programs can provide pupils with some helpful ideas as they begin to think about careers. There are not always sufficient opportunities for pupils to explore the suggestions with their guidance teachers.

- **Guidance staff should ensure that sufficient time is allocated to examine and analyse the information that pupils obtain from computer print-outs (6.4).**

11.11 Careers Officers provide an important service in interviewing and advising pupils about future careers. They are not always fully briefed on individual pupils' abilities and aspirations.

- **Guidance staff should always ensure that briefing information for Careers Officers is provided in advance of careers interviews (6.7).**

Personal guidance: individual support and counselling

11.12 Guidance staff are closely involved in providing support for individual pupils who have particular learning and/or behaviour difficulties or who are attempting to cope with personal crises or decisions.

- **Guidance staff should be closely aware of the specific circumstances of particular pupils. They should be in a position to contribute effective, well-targeted support in terms of pastoral, curricular and careers guidance (7.1 - 7.14).**

Education for personal and social development

11.13 Education for personal and social development is a whole-school responsibility. There are particular aspects of personal and social development which are most effectively promoted through specific PSE programmes. Often PSE is accorded low priority in terms of staffing and timetabling.

- **Schools should review and evaluate the extent to which PSE programmes contribute to the development of core skills (8.1 - 8.7).**

- **Senior management should review the priority given to PSE, and with guidance staff should evaluate the quality of PSE programmes (8.8 - 8.19).**

- **Schools should consider certificating elements of PSE (8.20, 8.21).**

Promoting partnership

11.14 There are many ways in which guidance contributes to the quality of the partnership which schools have with parents, support agencies, employers and post-school education.

- **Schools should evaluate the quality of their links with parents and all outside agencies (Chapter 9).**

Management and quality assurance

11.15 In order to meet the complex, numerous and wide-ranging needs of pupils, guidance provision in each school needs to be well managed and effectively co-ordinated.

- **Senior management and guidance staff should review and evaluate the management of guidance in their school, taking account of the references in this report to aspects such as: the management of staff and resources; the formulation and implementation of policies; and development planning in guidance. They should consider the use of performance indicators as tools for measuring quality (Chapter 10).**

Printed by HMSO Scotland
Dd 8403473 8/96 (130695)